THE INFLUENCE OF TECHNICAL COOPERATION ON REDUCING TENSIONS IN THE MIDDLE EAST

Robert B. Abel

University Press of America, Inc.
Lanham • New York • Oxford

Copyright © 1997 by
University Press of America,® Inc.
4720 Boston Way
Lanham, Maryland 20706

12 Hid's Copse Rd.
Cummor Hill, Oxford OX2 9JJ

British Library Cataloguing in Publication Information Available

Library of Congress Cataloging-in-Publication Data

Abel, Robert B. (Robert Berger).
The influence of technical cooperation on reducing tensions in the
Middle East / Robert B. Abel.
p. cm.
Includes bibliographical references.
1. Jewish-Arab relations--1973- 2. Water resources development--
Middle East. 3. Regional planning--Middle East. I. Title.
DS119.7.A6176 1997 338.956--dc21 97-54912 CIP

ISBN 0-7618-0698-9 (cloth: alk. ppr.)
ISBN 0-7618-0699-7 (pbk: alk. ppr.)

Dedication

By common consent, this book is dedicated to the memory of President Anwar El Sadat of Egypt, who was the first to begin bridging the gap between Israel and its Arab neighbors. It was his immortal speech to the Knesset that set the stage for the Camp David agreements, of which the Cooperative Marine Technology Program was the initial product.

Second, I would be remiss in failing to recognize the significant contributions to Middle East Peace of two extraordinary gentlemen: The late Prime Minister General Itzac Rabin, who, as a modern Moses, led his country—and the region—from a wartime to peacetime condition; and Rear Admiral Yohay Ben Nun, father of the modern Israeli navy, who first helped me conceive the Cooperative Marine Technology Program in his Washington, D.C., hotel room. He was a hero in Israel and an inspiration to me. His tragic death last year was a terrible loss to our community, all members of which respected him professionally and loved him personally.

Contents

Preface

Most treatises on social and natural sciences commence with a common complaint relating to the scarcity of previous work and available data. The following document confronts precisely the opposite situation: an overabundance of previous writings and an overwhelming body of thought on the general subject of tension reduction in politically sensitive regions. This is particularly true of the Middle East, where hundreds of social scientists in all categories have applied their experiences and talents to the problem of bringing about peaceful solutions in the war-torn area.

A second feature differentiating this study from others of its kind relates to a shift in doctrine in the agency mandated by Congress to sponsor and supervise such programs. Specifically, the Agency for International Development (AID) has partially shifted emphasis from the use of technology to advance cooperation to excellence per se of the science and economic development. Analysis of the shift and its effects has broadened the scope of this monograph beyond that of other works on the subject.

I wish to recognize the United States Congress, which spawned the Regional Cooperation Program, and the Agency for International Development for its sponsorship, as the implementing agency, over the past fifteen years. Thanks must also be rendered to the Hanson, Rockefeller, Dorot, and Scheuer Family foundations for their assistance. Finally, I wish to express my appreciation to Ambassador Sam Lewis, former president of the United States Institute of Peace, and his colleagues, who sponsored the preparation of this document.

This book was conceived by an Egyptian member of the Steering Committee of the Cooperative Marine Technology Program for the Middle East, Counsellor Ahmed Al-Ibiary, then executive officer of the Egyptian Academy of Scientific Research and Technology. He first voiced the concept for the book at a meeting in Haifa in March 1991, and progression from concept to outline, writing, and review has occupied the ensuing months. The perspective in which the Egyptians suggested this writing is, in their own words:

> The Middle East has long endured the calamity of war and hatred. It
> is not natural that life should continue under the threat of arms and
> souls full of hatred. Consequently, it was inevitable that efforts be

exerted to find a solution which could bring security to the area and safety to the world as well.

Scientists in this region, particularly those interested in the fields of oceanography and fisheries, were not far from the scene. As they saw it, science is universal in nature and marine studies cannot be integrated without international cooperation, and in particular, the cooperation of border countries in completing studies of the marine environments that their political borders share.

Beyond the international movement was the peoples' readiness and willingness for peaceful coexistence supported by capabilities and powers available for their welfare, instead of wasting them in disputes leading to destruction and underdevelopment.

Associated with the initiative by the late President Anwar El Sadat in 1979 was the first attempt to bring about an international program called the Middle East Marine Technology Program. Egypt was the first country to respond to this initiative.

This initiative and response could not have continued for the next fifteen years without the financial support of the U.S. Agency for International Development, which allocated the funds to hold the meetings and workshops cooperatively among Egypt, Israel, and the United States and to support topical researches to be implemented in the three countries (joined in 1986 by Jordan) whose scientists exchanged results in workshops organized for this purpose.

AID's policy achieved its goals, as evidenced in the scientific results attained, friendships which prospered, and common good faith which remained as the program's hallmark through its career, to this day.

But we cannot forget the pioneers who participated and dedicated their efforts to the task regardless of the difficulties they confronted at the beginning. Thus, it is all the more pity that so few of them have lived to see the harvest resulting from the seeds they spread with such good will. They are, in Egypt, the late Professor Dr. Eng. Hassan Ismail, President Sadat's minister of science and higher education; Professor Dr. Abdel Fatth Gohar, Egypt's "guru" of marine science; Professor Dr. Abdul Fotouh Abdal Latif, president of the National Academy of Scientific Research and Technology; and Professor Dr. Ahmad El Rifai Bayoumi, director of the National Institute of Oceanography and Fisheries. Still active in the program is Counsellor Ahmed Ismail El Ibiary, and still active, but retired from the program, is Dr. Ahmed Mohammed Eisawy, former director of the National Institute of Oceanography and Fisheries, and Dr. H.K. Badawi, his successor.

In Israel, Rear Admiral Yohay Ben Nun was my original partner in conceiving the program. At the time he was director general of the Institute for Oceanographic and Limnological Research, later becoming its board chairman. He was succeeded by Dr. Collette Serruya, who is now special consultant to the Jewish Agency for Water Affairs. The current director general is Dr. Yuval Cohen, who is also Israel's representative on the Steering Committee.

In the United States, strongest support came directly from the Congress, in particular from Senator Claiborne Pell, chairman of the Senate Committee on Foreign Relations; Representative Henry Waxman, author of the amendment of the foreign assistance legislation that established this program; and Representative James Scheuer, without whose willingness to do battle for us in both the executive and legislative branches of government, we would have faltered long since.

Finally, special honor must be rendered to Dr. Sayed Zechariah El-Sayed, my partner and highly esteemed colleague, who has served as chief scientist of the program since its inception, and accepted the role of principal investigator upon my change of assignments.

The program is about to pass its fifteenth year of operation. This book has been prepared to record the history of an experiment accomplished under circumstances many of which were not beneficial to its protagonists. Its successes, therefore, include not only the technological achievements, but improved and shored-up infrastructures in the participating nations, thus paving the way for all of the cooperative programs that have and will follow.

1. Introduction

Examination of the Relevant Literature

Every Sunday school student has been exposed to the story of tension in the Middle East, site of the oldest continuing strife in the record of civilization. Yet our generation is privileged to witness what may be the first achievement of stability in all the history of that region. Paradoxically, this appears to be occurring during a period when large sectors of the world are undergoing societal dismemberment.

The mountainous mass of literature relevant to this situation, which is being published at an exponentially increasing rate, bears testimony to the importance of the Middle East peace process, whether viewed as an historical or geographic anomaly.

This report searches for a linkage between tension reduction and technical cooperation. The existing body of literature, however, does not treat this subject with much respect. In recognizing that "a reduction in tension ... between Israel and its neighbors is of paramount importance to the entire region," Eliyahu Kanovsky discounts most of the "hope" factors as unrealistic. Thus he observes that "Israel-Arab technical 'cooperation' (a euphemism for technical aid), in agriculture, for example, has never amounted to much in the Egyptian experience; nor will technical 'cooperation' be the problem-solving magic elixir elsewhere." It is only fair to point out, however, that this seemingly pessimistic observation is only one in a series of six "debunking" assertions.[1] In addition, Patrick Clawson, editor of *Orbis* and resident scholar at the Defense Institute for Strategic Studies, avers that technical cooperation by itself cannot be effective, primarily owing to lack of enforcement. He prefers a bricks-and-mortar approach in which all of the countries would have to use some sort of facility (e.g., an airport) in common.[2]

In "The Limited Scope for Economic Cooperation in the Contemporary Levant," his comprehensive contribution to *The Arab-Israeli Search for Peace*, however, Dr. Clawson pays careful attention to cooperative derivation and utilization of water and energy. He suggests that "the most extensive form of cooperation would be a free flow of labor and capital, integration of utilities (like electricity and telephones), common transport facilities (including full development of Gaza Port and joint use of Lod and Amman airports), and a monetary union." Bringing his subject close to home, he states, "Aid has been poorly used in the past to subsidize inappropriate investment, failing state companies, and food subsidies...."[3] This may provide a clue to AID's antipathy toward mariculture as an important medium of technical cooperation.[4] And, in the same report, Dr. M.Z. Diab omits technical cooperation from the seven steps he suggests "might be taken to minimize tension...."[5]

In what may be the most sophisticated assessment (if the prestige of the participants is an acceptable index of measurement), the final report of the Washington Institute's Strategic Study Group, "Pursuing Peace: An American Strategy for the Arab-Israeli Peace Process," devotes 52 pages to an analysis of peace efforts and the recommendations stemming therefrom. However, only half a page is devoted to technical cooperation, including water issues, pollution in the Gulf of Aqaba, air traffic control procedures, electricity load sharing, and fiber-optic cables.[6] The Institute director, Dr. Robert Satloff, explains that technical cooperation is a micro-issue, and thus simply not within the range of discussion at that particular level of participation.[7]

Geoffrey Kemp of the Carnegie Endowment for International Peace and an Institute participant agrees that technical cooperation is nice but lacks the clout of economics and disarmament as the dominant issues.[8] Graeme Bannerman of Bannerman Associates, on the other hand, wonders in retrospect why the subject did not receive more recognition. Dr. Bannerman was a particularly strong supporter of the Cooperative Marine Technology Program during his tenure as chief of staff of the Senate Foreign Relations Committee.[9]

In one of the best-articulated contributions to the literature on reducing tension in the Middle East, Ambassador Samuel Lewis and Dr. Kenneth Stern offer a guidebook for the management of any program involving Israelis and Arabs. Some of their recommendations relate critically to the Middle East Regional Cooperation (MERC) Marine Program, especially in its more recent history:

> ...[M]ediators should facilitate, not dominate, the negotiating process.
> ...[M]ediators cannot rush the parties to a conclusion.
> Avoid becoming embroiled in ... domestic politics.[10]

Change "mediators" to "principal investigators" and you have a basic triad for educating a prospective Cooperative Marine Technology Program Director. More recently, in a discussion on October 14, 1994, at the Plaza Hotel in New York, Ambassador Lewis added the observation that as the factors discussed herein gradually catalyze the peace process, those fundamentally opposed to this process will expand their efforts to disrupt it.

The rapidly increasing attention being given to regional cooperation in the Middle East made inevitable the birth of a periodical devoted to the subject. The *Bulletin of Regional Cooperation in the Middle East* emerged on March 1, 1992, originally under the dual title "Bulletin of Regional Cooperation in the Middle East" and "Search for Common Ground." Volume 2, Number 1 purified the title, eliminating "Search for Common Ground."[11] The publishers have done a good job of confronting and compiling the avalanche of literature on the subject. Examination of the component articles leads to wonderment that there remain any new or underutilized words or phrases on the subject.

In introducing their massive review of cooperation and integration in the Middle East, Andrew Watson and Linda Northrop call attention to the more than four decades of efforts by various rulers, bureaucrats, and technicians to promote some sort of cooperation among the countries in the Middle East, but the record is largely of failures. They point out the obvious, i.e., the animosity and mistrust that ensued between Israel and its Arab neighbors from the foundation of Israel in 1948. They note the almost unique case of the Camp David talks with respect to communication between Israel and Egypt, which subsequently enjoyed diplomatic relations.[12]

It was then-governor Thomas Kean of New Jersey who pointed out in a press conference in October 1980 that the establishment of the MERC Marine Program was the first and only outcome of the Camp David agreement of several years previous. Now, of course, these communications have accelerated at an almost exponential pace.[13]

Watson and Northrop also suggest that a fundamental reason for the failure of the Arabs to integrate and cooperate may be their lack of complementarity. The evidence for this statement is that Arab countries trade mostly with the outside world, rather infrequently with one another, and not at all with Israel. One wonders whether a more important reason may be that there are few material items for the Arab countries to trade with one another. This becomes clearer if one sees that oil is nearly the entirety of Arab countries' exports. Oil revenues, however, as Watson and

Northrop point out, did not bring about cooperation between the Arab states and Israel. The exception may be the payments made by the oil-rich countries to the occupied territories, which may have indirectly assisted the Israeli balance of payments and the Israeli economy.

Watson and Northrop's analysis refers to a House of Representatives Committee on Foreign Affairs subcommittee report on Israeli-Egyptian research teams cooperating in entomology, bone diseases, marine sciences, and arid land development. Actually, in 1986 the marine program had been in action for over half a decade and the Cooperative Arid Lands Research (CALAR) was just achieving full speed. The case studies examined suggested that a few private Israeli entrepreneurs had at best limited success in opening up Egyptian markets in a cooperative manner, but the Egyptians didn't attempt the reverse process.

Finally, Watson and Northrop offer a fundamental differentiation—one that will be utilized and repeated often in this monograph—and that is the difference between talk and action. Their first category includes "a mix of activities such as think tanks, brainstorming sessions, conferences, education programs, writing, lobbying, diplomatic efforts, and the like, all directed to a variety of audiences." The second category, action, relates almost entirely to the projects reported to Congress as previously mentioned. Watson and Northrop recommend much more concentration on institutional activities such as legal processes, exchange controls, financial assistance, and other forms of economic cooperation. They believe the other topics (which are the focus of this monograph), such as food, water, and the sharing of other resources, to be unpromising because they are so close to the security of the individual countries that they will impede rather than encourage greater cooperation.

The famous Moscow conference of October 21–24, 1991, gave little space or time to technical cooperation vis-à-vis economic cooperation; this followed Watson and Northrop's recommendations for institutional types of projects. Nevertheless, the working group on economic cooperation did present a variety of projects in the guise of investment propositions, such as pipelines to carry natural gas from Egypt or oil from Saudi Arabia to Gaza, fertilizer and energy complexes on the Dead Sea, and a joint seaport and airport for Aqaba and Elat.[14]

In his article "Regional Cooperation in the Middle East," included in the *Arab-Israeli Search for Peace*, Gideon Fishelson uses his imagination in treating a natural gas pipeline from Egypt to Israel; an oil pipeline from the Persian Gulf to Gaza; a fertilizer plant; joint ventures in textiles and clothing; tourist packages covering the entire Middle East, including accommodations and guides; the production marketing of winter fruits, vegetables, and flowers; cooperation in transport services by land, air, and sea; and cooperation in providing high quality health services. It is interesting to note that in covering what he apparently believes to be the entire spectrum of human activities, Fishelson ignores the earliest MERC program relating to marine technologies. Nonetheless, he employs considerable knowledge and logic developing these suggestions, a complete explanation of which is beyond the scope of this book. He also discusses cooperative energy projects such as linking the electricity grids of Egypt, Jordan, and Lebanon; setting up a joint Israeli-Lebanese hydroelectric plant; and creating a Red Sea-Dead Sea water canal serving the hydroelectric and desalination plants that would be placed along it.[15]

In agreement with Watson and Northrop, Shafik Gabr of Arab Trade Organization for Cooperation (ARTOC) also deplores the lack of intraregional trade within the Middle East, noting that this trade amounted to less than 10 percent of these countries' exports, compared with 60 percent for the European Community and more than 30 percent for all developing countries. Gabr is somewhat more optimistic than most of the writers about the prospects for intraregional trade and economic cooperation. His reasoning relates to the availability of human resources, an investment base of over $400 billion, and relatively moderate infrastructure. He joins with Peter Goldmark in proposing some sort of regional "authority," in this case a financial institution and economic commission that would promote cooperation from both administrative and financial viewpoints. He also suggests establishment of a Middle Eastern business development center, which would be a nongovernmental nonprofit organization bringing together professionals from all the countries. This center, according to Gabr, would have branches in Israel, Egypt, Jordan, Turkey, and Palestine and would facilitate financial, economic, and technical cooperation, the latter through such means as cooperative data banks.[16]

Several other countries, in attempting further enhancement of Middle East technical cooperation, have captured the spirit of a regional authority or center. For instance, as reported in the spring 1994 edition of the *Bulletin of Regional Cooperation in the Middle East*, Japan, as chair of the multilateral working group on the environment, has pledged $530,000 for establishing a regional center devoted to the environmental protection of the Gulf of Aqaba and for a project to prevent desertification. Japan has also suggested the establishment of some sort of consultative group to establish a code of conduct for the protection of the environment by all the countries.[17]

According to Gabr, the two areas of most immediate promise for cooperation are tourism and infrastructure (transport and communications). With respect to tourism, Gabr jibes with Clawson and others who recognize the enormous financial benefits to all of the Middle Eastern countries in common from tourism. As will be noted in the last chapter, I agree wholeheartedly but invite attention to the technical aspects of enhancing tourism, which in themselves require cooperation among the Middle Eastern countries.[18]

In recommending objectives for technical cooperation, Dr. Benjamin Gaon from Coor Industries uniquely identifies "cement" for bonding relationships among the Middle Eastern countries (the obvious pun is almost impossible to avoid). He also agrees with others in suggesting telecommunications, petrochemicals, and the light food industries. He uses Coor Industries as an example of a large industry (perhaps Israel's largest) that is committed to long-term strategic partnerships on a regional basis. In addition, he raises the possibility of giving Palestinians access to Coor's commercial network abroad in order to promote Palestinian industry to third world countries. This network includes 20 offices around the world and an established system for landing the crucial export contracts the Palestinians so desperately need.[19] It is rather difficult to understand why almost none of the writers in this field pay any attention to fishing technology as an opportunity for intercountry cooperation. There appears to be no question of the need. According to Dr. Salaama Shakar, consul general of Egypt in Washington, D.C., Jordanians need fish very badly and are extremely eager to cooperate in such matters.[20] According to the president of the Egyptian Academy of Scientific Research and Technology, Dr. A.A. Latif, Egypt projects a need for four hundred thousand tons of farmed fish per year by the end of this decade, and, according to a number of Israeli officials, fish cultivation ranks extremely high on their list of priorities.[21]

It is expected that environmental considerations will rapidly increase, possibly outgrowing all other considerations except that of fresh water in stimulating technical cooperation in this region. For instance, according to Philip Warburg, director of the Environmental Law Institute's Middle East program, Israel currently draws 22 percent of its water from the so-called Mountain Aquifer, which underlies major portions of the West Bank and Judaean Hills. Contamination from untreated sewage, poorly regulated pesticide use, and disposal of hazardous waste threatens the aquifer's viability and poses a threat both to Israel and the Palestinians. Other movements for a common authority spring from the Cairo meeting in 1993, where delegates endorsed a plan for the establishment of a Palestinian environmental protection authority. At that time, Austria recommended an environmental data bank for the same region. In February 1993, the Environmental Law Institute, under the direction of Philip Warburg and Toby Bernstein, issued a monumental work entitled *Protecting the Gulf of Aqaba: A Regional Environmental Challenge.*[22]

In preparing this report the institute had received major assistance from the Adam Tevah V'din or Israel Union for Environmental Defense, the Arab Office for Youth and Environment in Egypt, and the Jordanian Society for the Control of Environmental Pollution. It would be hard to identify a better example of regional cooperation than evidence provided by this volume. In posing a challenge for cooperative technology, Dr. Mohammed Wahbeh concluded that "if the nations surrounding the Gulf of Aqaba and concerned parties in the international community cooperate and plan now, it should be possible to preserve the unique ecosystems of the gulf and to guide future development in harmony with the environmental restraints of the region. To accomplish these goals a major commitment is necessary, including tasks directed mainly at preservation of the aquatic environment but also relating to other aspects of societal activity."[23]

In the same book, Roy Mann discusses the need for cooperation on recreation and tourism. (Unfortunately he uses as an example the cooperation between Canada and the United States who, he explains, were "once at war with each other (War of 1812)," which is a misstatement inasmuch as Canada did not exist as an independent nation at the time.)[24]

Possibly the most thoughtful and incisive treatment of tourism, including both its intent and its technologies, has been rendered by Dr. Patrick Clawson in his Research Memorandum Number 26, "Tourism Cooperation in the Levant," completed under the auspices of the Washington Institute in May 1994.[25] Clawson quotes Israeli foreign minister Shimon Peres lamenting the fact that "the region has not fulfilled its potential for tourism" and contending that "the root of the problem is violence."[26] There would seem to be in this case a strong inference regarding the opportunities for useful technical cooperation in matters such as security protection. This would have particular meaning for communications technology, for instance. Clawson's overall theme relates to the power of tourism to demonstrate the rewards of peace and to forge cooperation between Israel and her neighbors. He follows with the realistic note that "however economically sound, regional cooperation must generate additional tourism, rather than redistributing existing visitors."[27]

During a visit to Jordan in 1990, a congressional delegation led by U.S. Representative James Scheuer and including the author tried to persuade King Hussein to remove the boundaries between Eilat and Aqaba to permit the sizable tourist contingent in Eilat to visit Petra in Jordan. At that time the king was willing in principle but hesitated for obvious political reasons. Dr. Clawson, however, pointed out that Jordan actually would not profit from the tourism from Eilat unless tourists extended their stays, because a one-day visit to Petra from Eilat would enrich Israeli hotels at the expense of Jordanian facilities.

Clawson's prediction proved quite accurate; in August 1994 the Jordanians agreed to lower the barriers but imposed the condition that visitors spend at least one night in Jordan.

At least in some quarters, Egyptian officials have been enthusiastic about the prospect of technical cooperation with the Israelis on tourism; in the governorate of Hurgada the governor was heard to discuss the prospects of coordinating a continuous recreational beach from Elat at least through Nueba in Egypt. He termed this a Red Sea Riviera, which the Egyptians look forward to establishing without the mistakes made in the original Riviera. (Incidentally, this discussion took place at a reception given in honor of the Israeli team visiting Hurgada under the auspices of the MERC Marine Program.)

Clawson also refers to cooperative technology for artisans and suggests that "the most promising peace-driven projects are in the Aqaba region, focusing on environmental cleanup, port relocation, and a jointly administered airport.[28] In personal conversation, Clawson has been quite explicit in stating that forced technical cooperation would be far more effective than voluntary cooperation. He cited as an example his concept of a common Jordan-Israel-Egypt airport using the same flying facilities, perhaps with three different entrances. This concept has the initial advantage of enforcing the use of the most modern technology as a simple matter of financial survival. Clawson also offers some rather surprising statistics in light of the fact that Israel, especially Eilat, is known as the Scandinavian Miami. He demonstrates that Amman has more hotel rooms than West Jerusalem and that there are more hotel rooms on Nile River cruise boats than in Tel Aviv and West Jerusalem combined.[29]

Summarizing the advantageous aspects of technical cooperation in the recreation and tourism industries, it would seem that the substitution of peace for a wartime economy would allow the acquisition and growth of wealth. Most certainly, revenues are increased by recreational travel (and, in fact, business travel as well). However, such industries as coral reef protection and preservation; aquaria (including underwater aquaria); beach restoration, preservation, and control; transportation and communication networks; and, of course, marketing will all benefit from regional cooperation.

On the one hand, Clawson warns that the tourism market offers "few incentives for regional cooperation" because recreational visitors don't travel around much. He notes the dominance of the package tours that leave travelers in one place rather than carrying them around. It seems to the author that this is simply a challenge to better marketing rather than a built-in deterrent.

Finally, Clawson suggests that while Israelis and Jordanians envision a degree of competition, the competitor that will probably become most advantaged is actually Egypt, owing to its much longer and unblemished shore. No one discusses the Saudi shore, which is probably more pristine than the others, due to an apparent policy of discouraging visitors.[30]

Another instance of the omission of technical cooperation as a valid technique of tension reduction was evidenced in "The Professionalization of Peacekeeping," a study group report issued by the U.S. Institute of Peace. While otherwise cogent, comprehensive, and extremely thoughtful, it at no point endorsed the use of, encouraged, or even enforced technical cooperation as a peacekeeping measure. Personal conversation with David Wurmser, the principal author of the report, revealed that this topic was barely discussed simply because it was of insufficient importance as a separate subject to the group convened for the study.[31]

This author is probably heavily biased in favor of technical cooperation as a result of my own experiences; after all, who among us is not guided by personal experience? Nonetheless, it sometimes is distressing that some of the greatest political and international thinkers of our era tend to ignore technical cooperation as a factor in reducing tension. For instance, as reported by the U.S. Institute of Peace in its *Contributions to the Study of Peace Making*, Volume 3, the American Academy of Diplomacy lists—via two conferences—10 features that characterize multilateral negotiations.[32] The listing is much too long for this type of monograph; suffice it to say that economic and technical cooperation were not included. In the same volume, "the distinguished Professor Harland Cleveland of the Hubert Humphrey Institute of Public Affairs in his *Birthday of a New World*" is quoted as asserting that there should be a new world agenda to make the world safe for diversity and that it should contain the following five components:

1. Radical disarmament and durable deterrence of nuclear weapons;
2. Deterrence of other exotic instruments of fear;
3. Organization to anticipate, deter, and mediate regional conflict, manage crisis, resolve ancient conflicts, etc.;
4. Strengthening of international systems for responding to humanitarian crises among countries; and
5. Development of a wider and more flexible system of world leadership—a "club of democracies" whose members are willing to act in different groupings in different situations in dissimilar regions pursuant to the purposes (if not always using the procedures) of the United Nations charter.

(Each of these components was followed by some explanatory notation for which there is insufficient room in this document.[33])

Nowhere in his "how to do it" catalogue has Dr. Cleveland mentioned anything about cooperation, whether technical, economic, or educational. Yet as a distinguished former university president and diplomat, Dr. Cleveland is in a position to recognize and evaluate technical cooperation as an instrument of tension reduction.

Of the hundred-odd conferences that have been convened to discuss accord in the Middle East, one of the most interesting took place on the campus of the University of California, Los Angeles, June 5–8, 1993. The participants were called together to investigate the practical possibilities for peace and cooperation in a region whose history is almost synonymous with war. As described by the Institute on Global Conflict and Cooperation of the University of California, San Diego, in its newsletter (Vol. 9, No. 2, Fall 1993), the conference included one of the most far-ranging mixes of participants in history, including scholars, specialists, policy analysts, and government officials—all of whom attended in unofficial capacities. The newsletter reported: "[F]ollowing the informal track-two method of statecraft—also known as citizen diplomacy—the meeting mirrored the official Middle East multilateral peace talks, with working groups assigned to examine the issues of arms control in regional security, water, the environment, economic cooperation, and refugees. As one conference participant put it, good intentions can go a long way in solving the most complicated and controversial problems. For example, American and European specialists suggested how programs developed in other regions could be adapted to the Middle East, and a number of Arabs and Israelis remarked how the opportunity for informal contact and impromptu conversation was highly productive. Such exchanges of course differ markedly from the often frosty and aloof conduct of the official talks."[34]

At this particular conference, the author was especially struck by the extremely informal, frank, and friendly attitudes of each of the participants toward the others. It was almost as if they all belonged to a fraternity, the main purpose of which was to chat about topics of common significance, representing the interests that had been assigned to them, and still maintaining the most open minds possible on each issue. As Dr. Steven Spiegel, the conference coordinator, stated, "[G]one are the old polemics and endless debates about obscure historical points. They are replaced by businesslike, even convivial, discussions about technical issues of mutual concern."[35] Technical cooperation threaded throughout the entire series of discussions and was recorded explicitly in the final plenary session.

The same Steven Spiegel, as editor of *The Arab-Israeli Search for Peace*, stated in his introduction that a barrier to technical cooperation is its irritation to powerful neighbors, but the demise of the USSR has reduced this as a factor. The Soviet withdrawal from the region has denied the radical regimes, such as Syria, their superpower patron and increased the influence of the United States. There is no question of the U.S. preference for technical cooperation, as expressed in the Waxman Amendment alluded to previously. In the same volume, however, Spiegel also states that the collapse of the Soviet Union could eventually lead to decreased U.S. support for Israel. But Secretary of State Howard Baker emphasized that it is after all the Arabs and Israelis who will have to live together, not the rest of us.[36]

Adam Garfinkle has accurately identified the imbalance between the Israelis, who sometimes appear to thrive on discussions of Arab-Israeli cooperation, and the Arabs, who are far more reticent and favor circumlocution.[37] In fact, on the few occasions that the Arab press leaked information about the MERC Marine Program, it has been in a most uncomplimentary manner and has thus provided all the more incentive for further reticence.

In the MERC Marine Program, however, almost the opposite is true. The Israelis, apparently sensitive to their Arab partners' position, carry reticence about the program almost to the point of fetish. On a certain occasion in 1990 when an Israeli university (that was not part of our program) published information concerning technical cooperation among Israel, Jordan, and Egypt under our program, an Israeli program participant took the university representative who had leaked the information to task in a manner politely described as vituperative.

In his introduction Garfinkle also invites attention to practical problems that would emerge attendant upon establishment of a semisovereign Palestinian state, such as water shortages, agricultural research, flies and mosquitos, and facilitation of pilgrimages to Mecca. He notes that these problems are not going to go away. On the other hand, the thinness of the dividing line between problem and opportunity is worth a bit of discussion. Certainly Garfinkle's prediction has proven to be true. But it's just these sorts of problems and the universal recognition of them that can promote, shape, and even accelerate technical cooperation in the Middle East, and technical cooperation can in turn lead to tension reduction. Furthermore, in an odd, paradoxical way, problems of a mundane nature can provide solutions to problems of a much more overarching nature. This idea will be treated more rigorously later in this document.

Of all the aspects of technical cooperation between Israel and Jordan, however, none is more dramatic than the coordination planned and/or executed respecting utilization of the Dead Sea and its resources. Discussions of the interrelationships between the two countries at all levels concerning the Mediterranean–Dead Sea Canal, Red Sea–Dead Sea Canal, resources, various desalination ideas, water treatment plants, and mineral recovery occupy many volumes. But that is another story and not germane to marine affairs.

Influence of the Water Issue

Without losing respect for the other technologies that are each, from their own perspective, essential to the continued development of Middle Eastern countries, there can be little question that water continually occupies the minds of those with the authority and responsibility to bring about peace. Water and its lack are equally visible.

This report is not just about water. However, the role of water supply in bringing countries to a point of technical cooperation requires at least a few representative references to relevant deliberations.

Almost from the birth of the state, Israel perceived water and/or its lack as an excellent basis upon which to build what Shimeon Amir calls a "dialogue of development" with third world countries in Africa, the Middle East, Latin America, and elsewhere in Asia. He notes that a quarter century after Israel obtained independence, it already had in operation 43 such projects.[38] Over the past decade, literally scores of conferences and studies concerned with water have taken place in the Middle East. Some of them went into considerable detail. For instance, the Armand Hammer Fund for Economic Cooperation in the Middle East, conducted during 1984–85, was one of the earlier discussions that predicted the doubling of demand for water in the Middle East by the end of the century, in this case with particular reference to the West Bank and Gaza.[39] (This is at some variance with the claim by Dr. Ramzi Sansur, chairman of the Department of Environmental Sciences, Bir Zeit University, that neither demand nor supply of fresh water need increase; the problem is overuse by societies other than the Palestinians.[40])

Noting that Israel draws its water from the same aquifer as do the Palestinians, the group recommended supplementing that source with water from the Nile, Litani, and Yarmuk rivers. They also noted Egypt's plans to irrigate the Sinai through a canal along the Mediterranean shore (described in several other publications). The most interesting statement, perhaps, is the claim by this group that Gaza, West Bank, and the Negev could all be supplied more cheaply by the Nile than from the Sea of Galilee (Kinneret); at the same time, this would release water from the Sea of Galilee for use in Jordan.

Not all students of Middle East problems consider water to be a likely agent of cooperation. For instance, in their heroic *Review of Literature on Economic Cooperation and Integration in the Middle East*, Watson and Northrop explicitly exclude water cooperation from their listing of cooperative research topics as being simply unpromising. According to these authors, water is so important that useful deliberation is unlikely owing to the stickiness of the several subissues.[41]

Gary Hoch offers tentative agreement with this thesis, referring to the water resource as the "region's most dangerous problem."[42] In analyzing the reasons for Syria and Lebanon boycotting the water talks, allegedly claiming the need to resolve their territorial dispute with Israel first, he suggested that in the Middle East, the word "territory" "often means water...." Whatever the reason, the boycott has hurt the talks generally, particularly as related by Dr. Munther Haddadin, chairman of the Jordanian delegation to these talks. Haddadin himself has admitted that even if an ideal relationship came about among the Palestinians, Israelis, and Jordanians, there would still be limitations in the resolution of the water issues—they are that sensitive.[43]

One of the farthest ranging conferences on the Middle East water crisis was held in Waterloo, Ontario, Canada, May 7–9, 1992. It was titled "The Middle East Water Crisis: Creative Perspectives and Solutions." Canada's deep and abiding interest in the Middle East water crisis was evidenced throughout the entire session and, as related by the Canadian minister for international development, Canada has committed her expertise and experience in hydraulic water management throughout North and South America, Asia, and Africa. Conference participants included representatives of most of the Middle Eastern governments; multilateral and bilateral peace talk participants; representatives from the World Bank, United Nations, and other international organizations; and a number of participants from various academic and other nongovernmental organizations.

Comprehensive description of the proceedings is beyond the scope of this paper, and certainly the problem has already been described in sufficient depth. Within this conference, however, Hisham Zarour and Jad Isaac of the Applied Research Institute of Jerusalem made an interesting case rather similar to that posed by Patrick Clawson, i.e., that realistic economics would reduce water usage in Israel, which is mainly through agriculture. They stated in clear terms that the government, which subsidizes irrigation, rather than the individual farmer was to blame for this problem.[44]

As an intriguing (if misleading) index of measurement of the proliferation of publications on the subject, the papers presented at this conference alone cited 159 references, very few of which were redundant. A calendar of international meetings, which followed the papers, listed exactly 50 conferences on water being planned for the year 1993. (Credit is due Dr. Glenn Stout of the University of Illinois for his work in the International Water Resources Association and for his conversations with the author, which helped to formulate many of the opinions herein stated.[45] Credit is also due Dr. Thomas Naff of the University of Pennsylvania, who has apparently compiled the largest bibliography on Middle East water problems in the world.[46])

At this point it should be interjected that water problems, and discussions, and posed solutions thereto, are hardly of recent vintage. Dr. Ulrich Kuffner of the World Bank discusses irrigation schemes in the Indus Valley in Mesopotamia and Egypt dating back thousands of years.[47] Dr. Douglas Inman of the Scripps Institution of Oceanography's Coastal Research Institute has on several occasions described the magnificent plumbing schemes in the Roman Empire, some of which are still visible in Israel today.[48]

Possibly the most "far out" scheme to surface over the past decade was inferred in the MERC Marine Program itself. It stemmed from an observation by some Israeli engineers, notably Dr. Gad Assaf, of an apparent correlation between the rate of energy interchange between ocean and atmosphere and the "storm effect" (actually, the aggregate amount of rainfall) to be expected over ensuing seasons. The suggestion was first advanced that if the correlation could be proven, it would be possible to forecast the rain-originated water supply over a year's time, with the obvious consequent benefits to agriculture, urban planning, etc.

The second suggestion offered was that if the forecasting technique in fact proved effective, the next and final step would be modification itself. This would be accomplished by lowering the sea surface temperature of the Mediterranean by approximately one degree Centigrade.

The project itself is described by George Mellor and Marco Zavaterelli in Chapter 4 of this book along with the other projects of the Cooperative Marine Technology Program. Suffice it to say at this point that the program never proceeded beyond the first stage owing to problems associated with instrumentation procurement under the prevailing regulatory environment. Actually, this concept is receiving increasing attention lately in the United States, Israel, and Turkey, and it will be interesting to note whatever momentum develops.[49]

One intriguing factor that has been noted in discussions in which the author has participated relates to the difference in perspective and approaches between engineers and economists. This was brought out explicitly by Alan Richards in his "Strengthening Markets to Build Peace: The General Case, Illustrated by the Example of Agriculture and Water." This paper was prepared for the Project on the Middle East Multilateral Talks, at the Center for International Relations of the University of

California, Los Angeles. Dr. Richards states specifically that "two features of water are debated in sensible discussion":

1. Water policy disputes are highly politicized; and
2. Analysis is dominated by engineers and technical experts, who too frequently neglect basic economic analysis.

Dr. Richards goes on to deplore engineers' domination of water issue discussion in Israel and the West Bank, which he feels to be largely the case throughout the world. His argument is that engineers tend to treat use and availability as if they were fixed quantities, varying only with the population for use or with rainfall for supply. In supporting Patrick Clawson's thesis, he advises that these discussions neglect the role of prices in the allocation of resources.[50]

In that particular conference Dr. Richards was followed by Sulayman Al-Quidsi of the University of California, Davis, who had collected some diverting statistics. Although his statistics and tables are beyond the scope of this report, his findings are interesting. In Jordan, for instance, the per capita annual water use is 173 cubic meters, vs. 447 cubic meters in Israel and 1,202 in Egypt! Second, water use as a percentage of total internal water resources appears to vary considerably, from 10 percent in Syria to 88 percent in Israel and 97 percent in Egypt. In noting the higher availability of water in Egypt, Dr. Al-Quidsi suggests that in the near future Egypt will also have a water crisis owing to population increase, and that this crisis can be rapidly exacerbated if in fact African countries such as Ethiopia carry out plans that would absorb more of the water of the Nile near its headwaters than at present.[51]

Peter Gleick reinforces Dr. Kuffner's historical analysis by discussing cooperation (or rather, the lack thereof) as far back as 2500 B.C., when conflicting city-states, instead of cooperating on irrigation water, fought by diverting it away from the other side. Apparently, destroying water supply canals and irrigation networks was a favorite hobby of early conquerors. He notes that perhaps the most bizarre example of Middle East cooperation in water occurred in 612 B.C. when a coalition of Egyptian, Median, and Babylonian forces attacked and destroyed Nineveh, the capital of Assyria, by diverting the Khosr River to create a flood.

Bringing his paper up to date, Gleick issues a passionate statement concerning the obligation of the Middle East nations to share water data and to resolve water-related disputes peacefully. He notes in particular the current activity of the International Law Commission in "considering adoption of a principle of participation that affirms the duty of all basin states to participate in the development, use, and protection of shared water resources." Finally, Gleick calls attention to oddball schemes that were laughed at a few decades ago but that are now being given serious consideration, such as the much-discussed diversion of icebergs from the Antarctic to the Middle East.[52]

Another factor—certainly on the pessimistic side—relates to the expense attendant upon almost all of the water supply solutions. This has been stated clearly by Dr. Jad Isaac, who ought to know: his Applied Research Institute had to close down temporarily in the summer of 1992—because it ran out of water! Isaac points out that nearly all of the technological solutions would cost almost a quarter of the annual per capita income of the Palestinians, which of course would force them out of the market.[53]

Joyce Starr has made a career study of the Middle East water resource crisis. Her classic, "U.S. Foreign Policy on Water Resources in the Middle East," was in a sense a clarion call to the United States to exercise the necessary leadership to bring all parties together to consider common solutions to their common water problems. Although the report was issued in December 1987 by the Center for Strategic and International Studies, the hoped-for results never actually took place, according to Dr. Starr.[54]

The Washington Institute for Near East Policy offered a material contribution to the literature in publishing "Water and the Peace Process: Two Perspectives," a parallel presentation including "A View from Israel" by Shlomo Gur and "A View from Jordan" by Munther Haddadin. Gur claims that "Israel has fully exploited the water resources of her territory and is presently in a regime of water rationing. She has reduced the water allotment to her farmers by 18% and is planning to recycle her waste water for agricultural use. According to Israel's Master Plan for water allocation in the year 2000, water for agricultural use will be reduced by 40% and water for domestic purposes will be increased by 52%. Israel, in other words, is on the verge of the water desalination era."[55]

Dr. Yonah Ettinger supports that plan, suggesting that all of the Middle East nations ought to consider in common a slight deemphasis on agriculture from 80 percent utilization of the available fresh water to 60 percent. This would double (from 20 percent to 40 percent) the amount of fresh water available for domestic consumption. This increase could be assigned to industry, tourism, fisheries, some combination of the above, or other uses.

Such an action would also align these nations more closely with the industrial nations. Furthermore, it would reduce waste, which is still a major factor in water conservation in several of the Middle East countries. Dr. Ettinger, formerly director of the Atomic Energy Commission of Israel, is science counsellor to the Israeli ambassador to Washington.[56]

Haddadin notes that water issues are posed in both the bilateral and multilateral talks and, if anything, "... water is needed to keep the talks alive and to have them bear fruit. Alternatively, water is capable of inflicting damage and devastation when floods are not controlled. In other words, by its very nature and occurrence water can promote fruitful cooperation, or may trigger and accelerate destructive conflicts."[57] While both of these experts agree that equitable sharing of shareable water resources is necessary, they naturally disagree on what is "equitable." They also agree, however, that the allocation of water resources is a very ripe field for regional cooperation and for support from developed countries.

In his article, Haddadin suggests that the objectives can be obtained through efficient water use, increased sophistication in plant production and animal husbandry, improvement of the harvest from rain-fed agriculture, and improvement of agricultural management systems. In this he ignores the possibility of deemphasizing agriculture in favor of mariculture, as is suggested elsewhere in this report, but, significantly, he accepted that thesis at the California conference previously reported.[58]

An interesting viewpoint is contributed by Dr. Patrick Clawson, who hews steadfastly to the argument that attaining an adequate and equitable water supply in the Middle East is simply a matter of efficient and effective pricing. In other words, by allowing the price of water to seek its own natural level, free of subsidy, the various groups involved will gradually converge on a universally optimum usage rate. Noting that the apparent problems of water shortage have led to fears that there simply won't be enough water to accommodate everyone, particularly including Soviet immigrants, and that political settlements will have to include steps to limit immigration, he replies that these claims are flat wrong: the water shortage does not mandate any particular settlement of the conflict. Water is by no means an insuperable barrier to the region's economic development and population growth. The water balance is primarily an issue of the price that supply and demand equilibrate. At a higher price for water, the demand would decline and recycling (e.g., of urban sewage) would become more attractive. In *The Arab-Israeli Search for Peace*, Clawson offers one of the few statements that make the case for reducing agricultural water demand, supporting Gur and Ettinger. He notes that cotton is basically solid water and that exporting cotton is in effect exporting potable water. His claim that ending cotton production would almost be sufficient to bring water demand to a level of sustainable supply has been borne out by informal discussion with other experts in the field.[59] When mariculture was proposed to AID (under the MERC Marine Program) as a means of conserving water among other things, the idea was mainly rejected.[60]

During the famous Moscow conference, however, all the participants on the water panel apparently agreed that emotion tends to overcome practicality. Furthermore, the inefficiencies of subsidizing water projects would be worth the price, if they would in fact be of significance in reducing tension in the region.[61]

It was at this same conference that the concept of an international authority to own the regional water facilities was first voiced in an international arena. As stated previously, it had been discussed four years earlier in conversation with Peter Goldmark, president of the Rockefeller Foundation. It was Mr. Goldmark who suggested that some sort of "authority" for the region, with particular reference to the Gulf of Aqaba, would go a long way to ensuring regional cooperation and reduction of tensions. At the time, however, he was referring to a much broader spectrum of activities than just water supply.[62]

When the concept was developed into a proposal for support under the Middle East Regional Cooperation Program, the Agency for International Development rejected its inclusion as a component of a cooperative scientific program on the grounds that it was politically beyond the scope of such programs.[63]

Viewing the myriad assessments of water as a factor in the Middle East on a chronological basis, one gets the impression of a paradox: as populations increase and the growth rate shows no immediate sign of stabilization, while potable water becomes increasingly scarce, the problem appears to be taken somewhat less seriously than in earlier years. For instance, in their study of "Israel's Water Policies" in 1980, Davis and Richardson concluded that Israel faced an almost terrifying water crisis, the causes for which related mainly to its territorial expansion and settlement policies. This cogent 30-page analysis treated both conventional (usage reduction, conservation) and unconventional alternatives (nuclear-powered water desalination apparatus, transfer from the Nile River, the Mediterranean–Dead Sea Canal, cloud seeding, and weather modification).

To tie all of the above together in a relatively coherent knot, a major objective of the MERC Marine Program was to solve the water problem by an altogether different means. This is best illustrated by the following logic:

1. Lack of potable water is acknowledged as the most serious common problem in the Middle East.
2. Seventy (some analyses range up to 85) percent of this water is absorbed by agricultural usage.
3. The alternative methods for water supply as described in the preceding paragraphs are uniformly expensive, and few have been proven by theoretical or model treatment.
4. Much of the agricultural productivity is for export; thus the export of cotton is essentially the export of potable water. Fruit and flowers may be similarly (though perhaps less seriously) categorized.
5. The only food item in the world not requiring potable water for survival and growth is marine fish.
6. Fishing in the wild presents many problems and drawbacks to the Middle East. In the first place, the Mediterranean Sea represents poor fishing grounds owing to oceanographic conditions; in the second place, what fish are there are traditionally caught by Spanish, Italian, Greek, and Turkish fishermen.
7. Because of this, the most obviously viable alternative to fishing in the wild is mariculture, or fish farming. In this instance semicontained aquatic areas are enhanced for fishing through the addition of fertilizers, and a number of programs are dedicated to producing increasingly cheaper feed for that purpose.
8. Therefore, the Middle East regional countries should reassess their priorities somewhat, reducing agriculture in favor of fish farming.

In summation, a major (possibly *the* major) intent of the MERC Marine Program has been to achieve optimum cooperation in all aspects of fish farming, the principal outgrowth of which would be water conservation and tension reduction.

Finally, it should be noted that it is only relatively recently that scientists, politicians, and scientist-politicians are tackling the sensitive subject of cooperative water conservation with enthusiasm and vigor. As pointed out earlier, of the more than 300 papers analyzed by Watson and Northrop in *A Review of Literature on Economic Cooperation and Integration in the Middle East*, few dealt to any degree with water.

(Author's note: Events involving technical cooperation in the Middle East are moving faster than the ability of the literature to stay apace. Thus, what began as a contemporary analysis will have been transmuted to a historical discussion by publication time.)

Notes

1. Kanovsky, Eliyahu, "The Mideast Peace Economic Dividend," *Middle East Quarterly* Number 2, 1994.
2. Personal interview with Patrick Clawson, June 24, 1994.
3. Clawson, Patrick, "The Limited Scope for Economic Cooperation in the Contemporary Levant," *The Arab-Israeli Search for Peace*, Ed. Steven L. Spiegel, University of California, Los Angeles, 1992.
4. Kenneth Prussner, in his letter of June 19, 1994, to Dr. Sayed El-Sayed, principal investigator for Phase IV of the MERC Marine Program, listed mariculture as a lower-ranking candidate for AID support.
5. Diab, M.Z., "A Proposed Security Regime for an Arab-Israeli Settlement," *The Arab-Israeli Search for Peace.*
6. "Pursuing Peace: An American Strategy for the Arab-Israeli Peace Process," final report, the Washington Institute Strategic Study Group, Washington, D.C., 1992.
7. Personal interview with Robert Satloff, August 3, 1994.
8. Personal interview with Dr. Geoffrey Kemp, June 24, 1994.
9. Personal interview with Dr. Graeme Bannerman, June 24, 1994.
10. Stern, Kenneth W., and Ambassador Samuel W. Lewis, *Making Peace Among Arabs and Israelis*, U.S. Institute of Peace, Washington, D.C., October 1991.
11. *Bulletin of Regional Cooperation in the Middle East*, a quarterly issued by Search for Common Ground, Washington, D.C.
12. Watson, Andrew, and Linda Northrop, *A Review of Literature on Economic Cooperation and Integration in the Middle East*, Center for International Studies, University of Toronto, 1991.
13. Press conference held by Governor Thomas Kean, October 1980, in Trenton, New Jersey.

14. Clawson, Patrick, "Building Toward Middle East Peace," working group report, *Cooperative Security in the Middle East*, Moscow, October 21–22, 1991.

15. Fishelson, Gideon, "Economic Cooperation in the Middle East," *The Arab-Israeli Search for Peace*.

16. Gabr, M. Shafik, "Promoting Regional Economic Cooperation in the Middle East: An Egyptian Perspective," Washington Institute Research Memorandum Number 24, January 1994.

17. *Bulletin of Regional Cooperation in the Middle East*, Volume 3, Number 1, Spring 1994, Search for Common Ground, Washington, D.C.

18. Clawson, Patrick, "The Limited Scope for Economic Cooperation in the Contemporary Levant," *The Arab-Israeli Search for Peace*.

19. Gaon, Benjamin, "Israel and the Future of Middle East Economic Development," Washington Institute Research Memorandum Number 24, January 1994.

20. Personal communication with Salaama Shakar, August 27, 1994.

21. Personal communication with A.A. Latif, December 20, 1993.

22. Warburg, Philip, and Toby Bernstein, Eds., *Protecting the Gulf of Aqaba: A Regional Environmental Challenge*, Environmental Law Institute, Washington, D.C., 1993.

23. Wahbeh, Mohammed I., "An Agenda for Scientific Research in the Gulf of Aqaba," *Protecting the Gulf of Aqaba*, Environmental Law Institute, Washington, D.C., 1993.

24. Mann, Roy B., "Tourism and Related Development Compatible with Aesthetic Resource Protection in the Gulf of Aqaba," *Protecting the Gulf of Aqaba*, Environmental Law Institute, Washington, D.C., 1993.

25. Clawson, Patrick, "Tourism Cooperation in the Levant," Washington Institute Research Memorandum Number 26, May 1994.

26. Peres, Shimon, *The New Middle East*, Holt & Co., New York, 1993, quoted by Clawson.

27. Personal communication with Patrick Clawson, June 24, 1994.

28. Ibid.

29. Ibid.

30. Ibid.

31. Wurmser, David, and Nancy Dyke, "The Professionalization of Peacekeeping," U.S. Institute of Peace, Washington, D.C., 1994.

32. *Contributions to the Study of Peacemaking*, Volume 3, U.S. Institute of Peace, Washington, D.C., 1993.

33. Cleveland, Harland, *Birthday of a New World*, quoted in *Contributions to the Study of Peacemaking*, Volume 3, U.S. Institute of Peace, Washington, D.C., 1993.

34. Institute on Global Conflict and Cooperation, University of California, San Diego, newsletter, Volume 9, Number 2, 1993.

35. Ibid.

36. *The Arab-Israeli Search for Peace.*

37. Garfinkle, Adam, *Israel and Jordan in the Shadow of War*, St. Martin's Press, New York, 1992.

38. Amir, Shimeon, *Israel's Development Cooperation with Africa, Asia and Latin America*, Praeger, New York, 1974.

39. *Overview of the Armand Hammer Fund for Economic Cooperation in the Middle East*, Ed. Haim Ben-Shahar, Seev Hirsch, Gideon Fishelson, and Meir Merhav. Tel Aviv University Press, Tel Aviv, 1986.

40. Samsur, Ramzi, remarks at Middle East Roundtable, UCLA, June 1993.

41. Watson, Andrew, and Linda Northrop, *A Review of Literature on Economic Cooperation and Integration in the Middle East*, Center for International Studies, University of Toronto, 1991.

42. Hoch, Gary, "The Politics of Water in the Middle East," *Middle East Insight*, Volume IX, Number 3, March–April 1993.

43. Haddadin, Munther, "A View from Israel," Washington Institute Research Memorandum Number 23, Washington, D.C., 1992.

44. Zarour, Hisham, and Jad Isaac, "Nature's Apportionment and the World Market: A Promising Solution to the Arab-Israeli Water Conflict," *Water International*, Volume 18, Number 1, March 1993.

45. Personal discussion with Dr. Glenn Stout, August 24, 1991.

46. Personal discussion with Dr. Thomas Naff, March 23, 1994.

47. Kuffner, Ulrich, "Water Transfer and Distribution Schemes," *Water International*, Volume 18, Number 1, March 1993.

48. Lecture given by Douglas Inman on August 23, 1980, at the Scripps Institute of Oceanography.

49. Mellor, George, and Marco Zavaterelli, "Numerical Study of Mediterranean Sea Circulation," *Journal of Physical Oceanography*, December 1993.

50. Richards, Alan, "Strengthening Markets to Build Peace: The General Case, Illustrated by the Example of Agriculture and Water," Project on the Middle East Multilateral Talks, Center for International Relations, UCLA, May 1993.

51. Al-Quidsi, Sulayman, "Water in the Middle East: Profile, Policies, and Prospects," Project on the Middle East Multilateral Talks, Center for International Relations, UCLA, May 1993.

52. Gleick, Peter H., "Reducing the Risks of Water-Related Conflict in the Middle East," Project on the Middle East Multilateral Talks, Center for International Relations, UCLA, May 1993.

53. Interview with Jad Isaac, conducted by Mark Perry, *Middle East Insight*, Volume IX, Number 3, March–April 1993.

54. Starr, Joyce R., and Daniel C. Stoll, "U.S. Foreign Policy on Water Resources in the Middle East," Center for Strategic and International Studies, Washington, D.C., 1987.

55. Gur, Shlomo, "A View from Israel," Washington Institute Research Memorandum Number 23, Washington, D.C., 1992.
56. Personal communication with Yonah Ettinger, August 26, 1994.
57. Haddadin, Munther, "A View from Jordan," Washington Institute Research Memorandum Number 23, Washington, D.C., 1992.
58. Institute on Global Conflict and Cooperation, University of California, San Diego, 1993.
59. Watson and Northrop, *op. cit.*
60. Ettinger, *op. cit.*
61. Watson and Northrop, *op. cit.*
62. Personal conversation with Peter Goldmark, president, the Rockefeller Foundation, May 8,1988.
63. AID letter of June 10, 1992, to University of Michigan.

2. Narrative of the Program

Congressional Stimulus

In contrast to most public (i.e., federal) programs in the United States, which are usually born in one or another federal government agency, the Regional Cooperation Program was initiated in the U.S. Congress, specifically in the U.S. House of Representatives, when Representative Henry Waxman of California offered the following amendment to the International Securities Assistant Act of 1978:

PUBLIC LAW 95-384 [S.3075]; Sept. 26, 1978

INTERNATIONAL SECURITIES ASSISTANCE ACT OF 1978

An Act to amend the Foreign Assistance Act of 1961 and the Arms Export Control Act to authorize international security assistance programs for fiscal year 1979, and for other purposes.

Be it enacted by the Senate and House of Representatives of the United States of America in Congress assembled, International Security Assistance Act of 1978.

SHORT TITLE

22 USC 2151.   SECTION 1. This Act may be cited as the "International Security Assistance Act of 1978".

CONTINGENCY FUND

22 USC 2261.   SECTION 2. Section 451 (a) of the Foreign Assistance Act of 1961 is amended by striking out "fiscal year 1978 not to exceed $5,000,000" and inserting in lieu thereof "fiscal year 1979 not to exceed $5,000,000".

"(5) It is the sense of the Congress that programs which stress regional development or regional scientific and technical cooperation between Israel and its Arab neighbors can contribute in an important way to the mutual understanding that must serve as the basis for permanent peace in the Middle East. Of the amount authorized to be appropriated to carry out this chapter for the fiscal year 1979, not less than $5,000,000 shall be available only to fund regional programs which stress development or scientific and technical cooperation between Israel and its Arab neighbors or programs which would be used for Arab-Israeli cooperation once normalization of relations between Israel and the Arab nations occurs.

The act (including the amendment) was signed into law by President Jimmy Carter as Public Law 95-384 of September 26, 1978.

Origin of the Program

For the first year of its existence, the law was not implemented, nor were the funds utilized. Then, during 1979, a small group of scientists from Egypt, Israel, and the United States worked toward establishment of an arrangement that would permit an elementary form of cooperation.

Prominent in this activity were Drs. A.R. Bayoumi, then-director of Egypt's Institute of Oceanography and Fisheries; A.I. El-Ibiary, executive officer of the Egyptian Academy of Scientific Research and Technology; Ismail Mobarek, of the University of Cairo; Hassan Ismail, then Egyptian minister of science and higher education; Admiral Yohay Ben Nun, director general of Israel's Institute of Oceanographic and Limnological Research; Ari Bach, assistant director general of the Institute; Sayed S. El-Sayed, of Texas A&M University; George Assousa, of the Carnegie Foundation; and Robert B. Abel, president of the New Jersey Marine Sciences Consortium.

A series of meetings in Haifa, Cairo, and Alexandria produced informal agreements to explore further the possibilities of cooperation in the ocean. By far the most significant achievement of these meetings was gaining the approbation of Dr. Hassan Ismail, President Sadat's brilliant minister of science and higher education. He gave the first "green light" for Egypt's participation.

A meeting between Dr. Abel and the Egyptian ambassador to Washington, Dr. Ashraf Ghorbal, produced the concept of the parallel bilateral approach. The fundamental characteristic of this approach was a

Figure 1. The Egyptian delegation, headed by Prof. Ahmed Mohammed Eisawy, the Director of the National Institute of Oceanography and Fisheries, consisted of nine distinguished scientists—the largest delegation of Egyptian scientists ever to visit Israel. The group included Prof. Hamed A.F. Gobarrow, an internationally renowned scientist and one of the founding fathers of Egyptian marine research.

series of identical projects between American and Egyptian institutions and (the same) American and Israeli institutions. The development of the concept and what it produced will be analyzed in Chapter 4.

A task force including Drs. Bayoumi, El-Sayed, Bach, and Abel spent a week during July 1979 to develop the first proposal (prospectively) under the aegis of the Regional Cooperation Program. It was submitted at the end of July to Mr. Blaine Richardson of the U.S. Agency for International Development. Mr. Richardson proved to be an able and dedicated advocate of the program. He was extremely helpful in our initial interactions between the group and AID, especially in convening the Review Committee under the leadership of Ms. Evelyn Keyes McMannes. The committee, following a meeting with Drs. Abel and Assousa, recommended full support of the proposal. It was initially rejected by the AID administrator on the grounds that the program was not desired by the Egyptians. This was proved to be a misunderstanding, however, by a cable from the ambassador to Cairo, Alfred Leroy Atherton, to Secretary of State Cyrus Vance. Thus, following some adroit maneuvering by Richardson and pioneering contracting efforts by Ms. Kathleen Cunningham of AID's finance bureau, the first grant was awarded, effective August 20, 1980.

From the beginning, the group recognized in the grant the necessity of restricting the program's goals to the fundamentals, i.e., food, health, and the protection of land from nature's aquatic forces.

The next major hurdle was convocation of all the prospective project leaders. Fortunately, the Richard Hanson Foundation in San Diego, California, was established to promote peace throughout the world. Dr. Robert Ontell, representing the foundation, was instrumental in arranging for the foundation to underwrite the expenses of that first conference.

Dr. William Nierenberg offered the full resources of the Scripps Institute of Oceanography to catalyze the meeting. Scientific leaders from Egypt and Israel met there with several Americans during August 23–30. A Steering Committee was formed on the first day, on a highly informal basis, to agree on a useful agenda.

The atmosphere of the first day's meeting was uncomfortable initially. In retrospect, the most surprising aspect of the conference was the speed with which friendships, alliances, and agreements were forged. The meeting ended on a spirit of resolve to challenge historical attitudes and overcome traditional hostilities. Perhaps this meeting was the first example of tension reduction in Middle Eastern affairs.

Participants in this meeting included the following:

Egypt	Israel	USA
A.A. Latif (Chair)	Y. Ben Nun (Chair)	R.B. Abel (Chair)
A.R. Bayoumi	H. Gordin	S.Z. El-Sayed
A.I. El-Ibiary	T. Berman	R. Drenner
A. Ezzat	G. Kissell	G. Assousa
S.H. Sharaf El-Din	G. Hulata	D. Inman
I. Mobarek	D. Adar	R. Ontell
M. Ishak	A. Golik	
M. Saad	M. Gophen	
H. Gohar		
A.Khafagi		

Figure 2. Israeli and Egyptian scientists at the Temple of Karnak, Egypt.

Goals and Objectives of the Program

The overall goal of the program was expressed in the enabling Act of Congress, i.e., to reduce political and social tensions in the Middle East by designing, promoting, and executing cooperative technical projects, the products and services of which would demonstrably benefit cooperating countries and organizations.

Social objectives toward those goals included the following:

1. Determining the respective nations' most pressing needs that were amenable to solution by marine activities. The most obviously important of these is, of course, marine fish because (as previously alluded to) humans have only one food product that does not depend on fresh water for survival and growth, and that is marine fish.

2. Identifying persons both technically competent and dedicated to peaceful collaboration.

3. Persuading responsible authorities in each country that the idea was worth exploring.

4. Providing motivation for scientists, especially younger people just entering the field, to cooperate with one another.

5. Expanding the spectrum of technologies to recruit new persons and organizations.
6. Making the program sufficiently successful to attract the attention of neighboring countries, and thus expanding the program geographically.

The following projects comprised the program.

1. Predictive Model for Shoreline Changes Along the Nile Littoral Cell
2. Circulation of the Eastern Levantine Basin
3. Induced Spawning of Grey Mullet
4   Experimental Feeding and Nutrition Studies of Some Brackish Water Fish
5. Coastal Management and Shore Processes in the Southeastern Mediterranean
6. Biological Productivity of the Southeastern Mediterranean in the Post-High Dam (Aswan) Period
7. Intensive Pond Culture and Fish Nutrition
8. Seafood Toxins
9. Lakes Management
10. Controlled Reproduction of Commercially Important Fishes
11. Technological and Public Health Implications of Wastewater Reuse in Aquaculture
12. Chemical Contaminants of Seafoods (Seafood Toxins)
13. Fish Nutrition
14. Development of Practical Diets for the Culture of the European Sea Bass *(Diecentrarchus labrax)*
15. Production of Monosex Tilapia

Progress of the Program

This program differs significantly from conventional AID programs in that, at least until recently, social progress (that is, cooperation among Egyptian and Israeli scientists and institutions) has been considered to be at least as important as the economic and intellectual accomplishments. A few highlights will serve to demonstrate.

1. By the end of 1994, the Egyptians and Israelis had conducted 33 joint planning and reporting conferences, mainly in Cairo and Alexandria to begin with, but increasingly in Haifa. More

recently, meetings have been held in Taba, to accommodate representatives of other countries and finally in Aqaba, Jordan. A full-scale workshop is held each year, in which all of the project's principal investigators participate. With a few exceptions, American participation has been limited to the role of program coordinators.

2. As of the same period, 50 Israeli person-trips have been made to Egyptian laboratories, where scientists have cooperated in research and have assisted in classrooms and with graduate students. Early visits to Israel by the Egyptian under secretary of state for aquaculture and the director of the Egyptian Coastal Protection Institute produced dramatic results. The latter, for instance, was appointed a consultant to the Israeli government in 1987. Since 1988, Egyptian project teams (6 to 10 persons) have regularly visited Israel, and teams of aquaculturists work frequently in the Eilat Laboratory.

3. The Israeli aquaculturists have entered an agreement to transfer technology, as it is developed, to a coalition of four kibbutzim (collectives), which have already entered into marketing arrangements with French and Italian consumers. Egyptian entrepreneurs are also exploring the possibilities of commercial aquaculture ventures.

4. Exchange visits by aquaculturists have resulted in sharing and utilizing data for accelerating growth of mullet.

5. Joint training of Egyptians and Israelis has been conducted in the United States under the Shore Processes and Tilapia projects.

6. Twenty students have obtained graduate degrees under the program's auspices, and their projects have generated more than 50 papers.

7. The Wastewater Utilization, Management, and Shore Processes projects produced the first coauthored publications.

8. An early highlight of the program occurred in 1983, when Dr. A.R. Bayoumi and Admiral Yohay Ben Nun (the original Egyptian and Israeli coordinators, respectively) were honored for their contributions to the program by being designated as the first co-recipients of the International Compass Award given by Compass Publications, Inc., and the Marine Technology Society for distinguished service in international marine affairs. In 1985, Dr. El-Sayed received the Distinguished Service Award from

the American Institute of Biological Sciences for his role in developing the program. In 1993, Dr. Abel received a similar award from the Egyptian government.

9. November 1988 marked another milestone in the program's career when a U.S. congressional delegation, led by Representative James Scheuer, met with the Israelis and a large Egyptian delegation in Eilat, Israel, to reflect upon the program's achievements and consider its future. Because of aquaculture's central role in Middle Eastern economic and technical development, the entire group then inspected Israel's National Mariculture Center. At that time, symbolic of the burgeoning Egyptian interest in the program, the nine-person Egyptian delegation (the largest yet to attend such a meeting) included Dr. Hamid Gohar, the pioneering leader of Egypt's marine program. His prominent role dated back to King Farouk's regime. Upon learning of his impending eighty-second birthday, the Israelis held a party featuring a gigantic cake. The emotional impact was enormous. (Tragically, Dr. Gohar passed away in 1994.)

10. A year later, there took place possibly the most significant meeting in the program's history, when Egyptians, Jordanians, and Israelis joined Drs. El-Sayed and Abel in Washington, meeting with—inter alia—the Deputy Assistant Secretary of State for Near-East Affairs, the chairman of the Senate Foreign Relations Committee, and Representative Schetuer, who had previously visited the program on site, as previously mentioned. Their delegations included Ambassadors Mustafa, Director of the Israeli Affairs Office of the Egyptian Foreign Ministry, and Zvi, Director of the Egyptian Affairs Office of the Israeli Foreign Ministry.

Management of the Program

The MERC Marine Program's outstanding advantage was its major disadvantage. Lack of precedent and guidelines (except for the congressional amendment itself) required the program's originators to proceed without assistance or guidance, but in so doing gave them a

Figure 3. Representative James Scheuer conducting an on-site investigation of the program's Mariculture and Environmental Protection facilities, Eilat, Israel 1988.

relatively free hand to "break trails." Accordingly, the author used the National Sea Grant Program as a general procedural guide, but deviated frequently and widely, in recognition of the interplay of social forces

The original proposal was prepared in two weeks. This fact merely recognizes the dedication and talent of the Israeli, Egyptian, and American collaborators, none of whom had ever attempted anything of this nature. The year occupied by AID in deciding to reprogram funds to support the program allowed for considerable correspondence among the persons who ultimately became responsible for the program's management.

Under the terms of the AID grant, Dr. Robert Abel, of the New Jersey Marine Sciences Consortium, was appointed principal investigator, with broad and largely unrestricted authority, except for his responsibility to the Consortium's president. When, in the following year, Abel became president of that corporation, the last fetters on his authority were removed.

This, however, was a situation where the relationship of the informal to the formal chain of command was obvious. Abel recognized immediately the need for ceding maximum authority (consistent with the grant's terms) to the collaborating nations, and within the year first encouraged formation of a permanent Steering Committee; then, as soon as appeared possible, formalized it.

Technical management of the program thus became largely the responsibility of its Steering Committee. More than any other aspect of the program, the Steering Committee reflects the spirit of cooperation so central to the program's success. It was also the first such organization formed under the aegis of the MERC Program. The Committee's functions originated on a relatively elementary level, but came to include the following:

1.   To stimulate thought toward project initiation in the three participating countries;
2.   To assist respective principal investigators in preparing their projects, including identifying partners in the other countries;
3.   To facilitate communications among the prospective partners;
4.   To screen the projects at first and second levels (this normally involves reducing 20 to 30 proposals to a package of between five and eight);
5.   To prepare the final proposal package, including management (proposals are generally prepared at approximately two-year intervals);
6.   To negotiate with the Agency for International Development;

7. To meet periodically with the principal investigators to assess progress and assist in the administrative phases;

8. To brief senior officials in the three participating countries on the nature and activities of the program; and

9. To prepare the final technical reports to be submitted each year.

In retrospect, it's not easy to understand why the Steering Committee worked so well. The simplest answer relates to the personalities, particularly of the Middle Eastern members. Except for their individual dedication, courage, and exceptional intelligence, the leaders' personalities are quite dissimilar. This is particularly important, considering that both the Egyptian and the Israeli contingents are under their third generation of leadership. Yet they are willing and able to come to agreement on all issues and priorities with extraordinary alacrity. Furthermore, since each enjoys a relatively high position and confidence at the ministerial level, they have access to national policy.

Until the Protocol (Appendix B) was agreed upon and cosigned in 1992, the committee obeyed no set rules; procedures were set ad hoc, by consensus. Membership was often expanded temporarily as additional or special expertise became needed. For instance, the chief financial officers of the Egyptian Academy and Israeli Institute attend most meetings, since budget and finance are perennial issues of moment. The Egyptian officer deserves special mention. Mr. A.I. El-Ibiary was the Academy's executive and finance officer until his formal "retirement" in 1993. He apparently continues to hold the position, de facto, and is the only Middle Eastern member of the Steering Committee to serve the program continuously from its inception. His keen insight into the political and managerial aspects of the program have proven invaluable over the years of its operation.

Support and Sponsorship of the Program

One of the more heartening aspects of the program has been the demonstrated high-level support. In Egypt, following Minister Hassan Ismail's original stimulus, the deputy prime minister, Yousef Walli, has been particularly outspoken in his support of intensified cooperation between the two nations generally, and with particular reference to the program. Successive Egyptian ministers of science and presidents of the Egyptian Academy of Scientific Research and Technology have expressed

Figure 4. Dr. Ahmed M. Eisawy (R), then-director of Egypt's National Institute of Oceanography and Fisheries, discussing mariculture plans with Hillel Gordin, Director of Israel's National Center for Mariculture, at Dr. Eisawy's new laboratory at Suez, Egypt.

the strongest possible support for the program. Dr. A.A. Latif, president of the Academy during 1989–92, not only supported the program but actively involved himself in its operation, chairing most of the workshop sessions. In Israel Prime Ministers Yitzak Shamir and Shimon Peres expressed their support for the program, with Mr. Peres displaying special enthusiasm for the principle In addition, Minister of Energy and Infrastructure Moshe Shachal strongly backed the program and also keynoted several joint sessions.

In the United States, support has grown within Congress, in the State Department, and in all of the American embassies in the region.

An important development in this program, whether considered in the category of natural or social sciences or both, relates to a recent subtle but significant shift in doctrine of the sponsoring agency, the Agency for International Development.

When the general manager of the program was given his initial assignment by the assistant administrator of AID for the Near East, Joseph Wheeler, he was mandated to utilize technology primarily as a tool to "make people work together." In other words, the primary purposes of the program were perceived by AID (and most certainly by Congress) as sociological and political. That this was a correct perception was verified by several members of Congress in both houses and in both parties and is reflected in their remarks in Appendix D.

During at least the first half of the eighties, this doctrine was scrupulously observed by both the active participants and AID. Regional cooperation was also very clearly the objective of the Hanson, Rockefeller, and Scheuer foundations, which supplied matching funds. During 1987–92, however, sponsoring philosophy changed somewhat. To technical cooperation and reduction of tensions were added the goals of scientific merit and economic payoff. This was substantiated in correspondence between the program manager and the assistant administrator of the AID Bureau for the Near East in 1991 and 1992, and elaborated in Appendix C.

It is not the purpose of this document to offer either approbation or opprobrium in this regard. It is necessary, however, to record that the shift in doctrine did, in fact, take place. In any case, it is worth noting that within the Steering Committee, opinion concerning the relative priorities was divided. The Steering Committee members from the research universities clearly favored the emphasis on scientific excellence. The general manager and his Middle East colleagues desired to adhere to the original motivation of the program, cooperation and tension reduction. Obviously, the key word here is "balance," because cooperation, scientific merit, and economic benefit are the three legs of the program "stool," which would collapse with the loss of any one of them.

Whether the ultimate purpose was justified or not, one outgrowth of the shift in emphasis related to the consummate care exercised by AID in its administration of the program. This was evidenced in the detailed attention and time given to research proposals and the protracted interchange of information among the proposers and project administrators. A vivid example of the care that AID exercised in fulfilling its partially modified mandate is portrayed in the following—a calendar of actions taken on the Proposal for Phase IV of the Cooperative Marine Technology Program.

Chronology of the Middle East Program
for Phase IV

June 6, 1990	Proposal for Cooperation in Fisheries/Mariculture, derivation of pharmaceuticals from the ocean, and trophodynamics of the Mediterranean submitted to AID

December 1990	Review committee meets on the proposal
Mid-April 1991	Review committee comments transmitted to the proposers
1st week in July 1991	The three countries react, form a new proposal, and submit it to AID
October 1991	Review committee reconvenes; comments referred back to the proposers, with more requirements
End of November 1991	Proposers reconvene, react to comments, and resubmit the proposal
January 1992	Proposers advised of impending new requirements that cannot yet be released
Late April 1992	Proposal amended as requested and resubmitted

Twenty-six months elapsed between submission of the proposal and conveyance of the funds to implement it. While probably in the government's best interest, in considering histories of somewhat visionary previous government grants and contracts, the impact of management of the program itself, particularly in terms of the original goals, was severe, including the following:

The Egyptian participants, clearly central to the overall goals of the program, had implemented their share of the program in good faith, recruiting scientists, setting up facilities, assembling instrumentation, etc. When they found that their investment of time and energy and particularly their political careers were jeopardized by cessation of the American promise, their alarm was evidenced in a flow of correspondence. Their threats to quit the program should have received greater attention than they did.

The Israelis also exhausted their funding but had planned their investments in a somewhat more flexible manner, which enabled them to switch the personnel assigned to the program to other ventures, thus diluting the effects of the deprivation of funding, but seriously impeding the program's progress.

The New Jersey Marine Sciences Consortium, as manager of the program, had to operate without compensation for a period of 17 months. This forced the organization to the brink of bankruptcy, from which it was saved only by the good faith of local banks.

Figure 5. The author briefing Prime Minister Peres.

Possibly the greatest loss occasioned by the deliberate proposal processing related to failure of the group to capitalize on opportunities offered by other Arab states to join the program. Here one traverses the boundaries between local allegiances and national and international policies of the involved nations separately and as a group. It requires no particular acumen on the part of the reader of an American newspaper to infer that it is in the best interests of the United States to achieve harmony and tranquility in the Middle East. It is also apparent that United States policy devolves closely on not only the nations with pro-American histories, but on the nations whose policies appear to be emblematic of the entire Middle East "attitude." These clearly include Jordan and Saudi Arabia.

The period 1990–92 represented, at least philosophically, a golden era in which the Egyptians declared that conditions should not be better for recruitment of Jordan and Saudi Arabia to the program. The participants were unable to capitalize on the previously mentioned letters of agreement because of what may seem to be a rather mundane reason—simply lack of funds to conduct the necessary meetings. Considering that the United States spends approximately $5 billion per year in the Middle East to "reduce tension," one wonders why approximately \$5,000, or 0.0001 percent of these funds, could not have been reallocated. The answer given was that AID was constrained by law to forbid use of its funds for travel to those countries because they weren't already in the program.

The preeminence and predominance of the Marine Program had been justified mainly in terms of its cooperative aspects. Its trail-blazing role was retained when during the early nineties it was still the only program with the promise of recruiting Arab nations other than Egypt. In this connection, it's worth noting that in the year following the Jordan peace treaty, two dozen proposals involving that country had been submitted to the agency. The Marine Program, however, remains the only enterprise in which the Saudi Arabians have expressed interest.[1]

Administrative and Political Issues

The unusual and pioneering nature of the MERC Marine Program has naturally raised a number of managerial issues. Many are common to all scientific programs; others are unusual, or even unique to this program. They will be analyzed in detail in Chapter 4, but the following summary is pertinent to the program's chronology.

At this moment, regional cooperation includes various programs in arid lands development, disease control, and agriculture, in addition to the Marine Program.

A crucial issue relates to the younger generation. One can't help but wonder whether program leaders have exerted the strongest possible effort under the circumstances to search for, identify, and recruit willing and competent graduate students into this program. While the cadre of eminent scientists who have chosen to devote their careers to peace in the Middle East is, of course, the *sine qua non* of the program, without whom we could never have gotten started, expansion to a recognizable regional effort must ultimately depend upon the next generation of young scientists.

A second issue concerns the relative importance of the Americans vis-à-vis the Middle Easterners in the program. The program began as a parallel bilateral operation with the American role dominant, because it was necessary to relate to the Egyptians and Israelis partly independently. As working relations rapidly improved, however, the trilateral aspects became more important, and, more recently, as excellent bilateral relations were achieved between Israel and Egypt, the American role has diminished and should eventually be reduced to that of consultants. In any case, regardless of how a project is organized at the start, the American profile is progressively lowered as the project develops.

The third issue relates to recruitment of other countries. Other nations apparently wish to join the program. Timing is important; attempting to rush these groups into cooperation with Israel will be self-defeating. It becomes increasingly useful to quietly demonstrate the value of cooperation in this region and the importance of substituting food for guns as a means of surviving in this part of the world.

Prospects for Internationalization

In 1990, the Egyptians dedicated their new Marine Sciences Center at Suez. This large complex encompasses laboratories dedicated to all facets of marine affairs, supported by the usual satellite structures, including docks, workshops, auditoriums, living quarters, etc.

Emblematic of the will of Dr. Latif, then-president of the Egyptian Academy of Scientific Research and Technology, to emphasize regional cooperation in this building, the first technical meeting held within its walls was that of our Steering Committee in August 1990. At that time, representatives of every institution in Egypt came to compare water problems and opportunities with their Israeli colleagues. Significantly, Jordan was represented at that meeting.

As previously mentioned, the Jordanians and Saudis indicated interest in the program by cosigning letters of agreement with the program's Egyptian cadre; the Aqaba Plan, when finally operative, will involve at least Jordan, and possibly Saudi Arabia.

Emergence of the Aqaba Plan

Until 1987, the Cooperative Marine Technology Program was largely confined to the Mediterranean Sea. The advantage related to the plethora of scientific and technological opportunities; the disadvantage was sociological in that cooperation was necessarily limited to Israel and Egypt. Turkey, Tunis, and Morocco expressed interest in joining the program, but were prevented by lack of funds.

In 1988, however, sparked by Dr. Khalil Hosny Mancy of the University of Michigan the group turned its attentions to another body of water. Here again, the program profited from divine intervention, which situated a valuable but environmentally sensitive bay in the midst of four nations, none of which usually speaks to one another. This is the Gulf of Aqaba.

In brief, the group first examined the socioeconomic prospects of a program that would feature research aimed at wise *development* of the Gulf's resources—mainly centered around mariculture—in combination with *protection* of its resources, mainly its celebrated coral reefs. The Egyptians quickly assumed a leadership role by cosigning cooperative agreements with the Jordanians and the Saudis similar to their arrangements with the Israelis.

At this point Jordan was invited to full participation on the Steering Committee, and the meetings were generally held in Egypt to permit Jordanian attendance. Agreement was quickly reached respecting technical objectives: mariculture, general oceanography of the Gulf, environmental monitoring, rapid response techniques for accidents, and aquatic recreation and tourism.

A proposal was prepared amalgamating the Israeli, Jordanian, and Egyptian aspirations. and submitted by the University of Michigan to AID in 1989. AID examined the proposal carefully and returned it several months later suggesting a number of modifications designed to make it more palatable, or better able to win support. Chief among these were deletion of the project on aquatic recreation and tourism (later targeted by the bilateral negotiating teams for emphasis); division into geographical sectors; and deletion of references to a "coordinating authority," which had originally been suggested by the president of the Rockefeller Foundation.

On the whole, AID's comments were cogent and relatively easy to incorporate. As of the end of 1993, however, the proposal had not been returned to AID in satisfactory style. This particular sad part of the program history is not germane to the purpose of this report. It is related only for the purpose of explaining how the Jordanians were recruited to the program and how their interests were able to merge with those of the Israelis and ultimately to contribute in a small way to tension reduction. Correspondence to the author from two successive directors-general of Jordan's Higher Council of Science and Technology are appended to this document to illustrate this point.

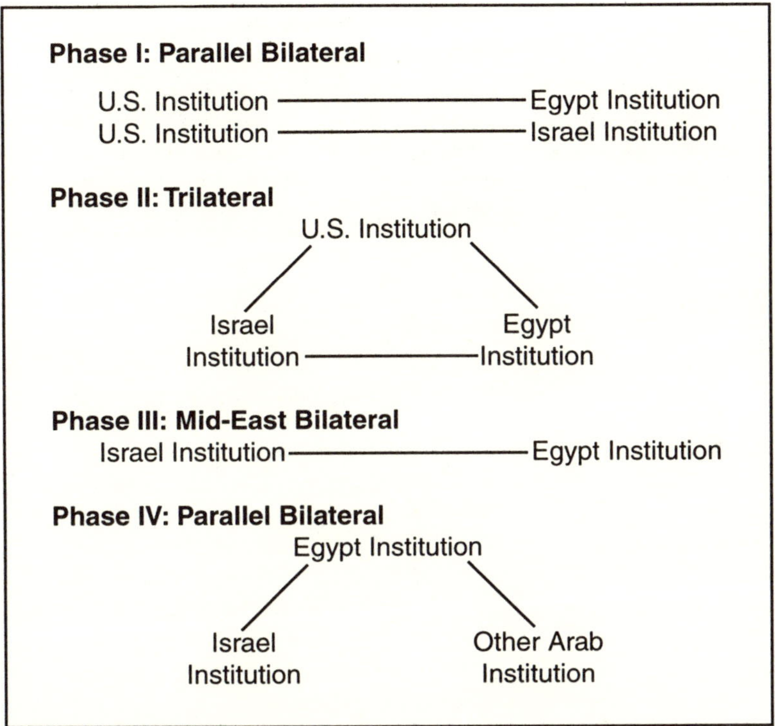

Figure 6. Depiction of the transitional phases of the Cooperative Marine Technology Program for the Middle East.

Summary of Progress

Generally speaking, the process moved forward in four major phases:

1. Establishing two identical parallel projects between an American institution and Egyptian and Israeli institutions, respectively; i.e., the "parallel bilateral" technique;
2. Bringing everyone together to form trilateral projects, initially de facto, and then de jure as the participants came to recognize the innocuousness of cosigning proposals and publications;
3. Diminishing the American institution's role, leaving Egyptian-Israeli bilateral projects; and
4. Revolving the entire system around Egypt, bringing in other Arab states. This is illustrated in Figure 6.

In summary, social gains seem to be self-catalyzing and progress to be exponential. Closer working relationships lead to better results. Better results awaken interest by scientists outside the program. The consequently improved recruiting opportunity offers more selectivity and more competent participation to the coordinators. Increasing competence leads to closer working relationships, better results, etc. In effect, the social machinery appears to be fueled by its own achievements.

Notes

1.　Letter of October 31, 1995, received from Professor Dr. Ohman Abdu Hashim, Dean of the Faculty of Marine Sciences, King Abdulaziz University.

3. Projects and Achievements

From its inception, the participants based their program on the fundamental needs of food, water, and land protection. Projects thus devolved to ocean productivity, seafood toxins, aquaculture/mariculture, waste water usage, shoreline protection, climate prediction, and lakes management. Teams of scientists and engineers from two dozen institutions in the three countries acted with the understanding that all projects would be conducted cooperatively. There was also general agreement that the Egyptian Academy of Scientific Research and Technology, the Israeli Institute for Oceanographic and Limnological Research, and the New Jersey Marine Sciences Consortium would be the coordination points. Texas A&M University collaborated with the consortium, and Dr. Sayed Z. El-Sayed of that university has acted as chief scientist of the program from its inception.

Organic Productivity of the Eastern Mediterranean

The Primary Productivity project sought quantification of the eastern Mediterranean Sea's capacity to sustain intensive fishing. The Haifa Institute and the University of Alexandria, assisted by Texas A&M University and the Bigelow Laboratory in Maine, conducted a series of cruises over the first six years. Those operations featured a complete suite of physical, chemical, and biological observations leading to intensive analyses of the phytoplankton (plants) and zooplankton (animals) populations.

The fundamental thesis underlying this project (as well as several others) relates to the naturally barren environment of the Mediterranean Sea. This region is characterized by hot, dry air blowing from the Sahara across the water, causing high rates of evaporation. The result is high-salinity water at all levels of the Mediterranean. This in turn causes water to be denser (by about 10 percent) than Atlantic water. Accordingly, the passage of water at the Straits of Gibraltar is characterized by the denser Mediterranean water flowing into the Atlantic, cascading to its natural density level at about 800 meters, and fanning out therefrom. The author has personally followed this water as far as Iceland, during a series of hydrographic stations taken in the early 1950s.

In turn, lighter Atlantic water flows on the surface into the Mediterranean. Owing to photosynthesis, however, water at the top layers of the Atlantic is almost totally devoid of nutrients such as phosphate, nitrate and nitrite, and silicate. This accounts for the nutrient content of the Mediterranean being approximately one-tenth that of the Atlantic Ocean itself at commensurate levels.

Then, the Aswan High Dam was completed in 1964.

In the past, nearly all of the nutrient input to the Mediterranean had been provided by the Nile River. Construction of the Aswan Dam, therefore, reduced the nutrient contribution to almost zero, with consequent destruction to marine plant growth. This in turn caused serious diminution of the grazers and, therefore, of the fish who subsisted on the grazers; in other words, the entire biological food chain was adversely affected by the dam. The purpose of the project was, first, to compare biological productivity of the southeast Mediterranean in the pre- and post-High Aswan Dam periods; and second, to quantify the effect of the nutrient reduction on fishing stocks.

This effect occurred in two stages: The first was an immediate decline in the catch of Sardinella Aurita, a planktivorous fish, which had an annual feeding migration to the Nile delta region during the pre-dam flood period. The cessation of the autumnal phytoplankton bloom in the post-dam period most likely resulted in an altered migration of the species to feeding grounds other than the Nile delta.

Second, following the immediate influence on the Sardinella, landings of larger fish declined in the late 1960s. While the obvious effect of the dam was most drastic and immediate on the fisheries of the delta, there is also evidence of abrupt changes in Israel's Sardinella stocks since construction of the dam, and, therefore, there is a strong likelihood of other, more gradual processes, all moving toward a trophic equilibrium.

The initial phases of the project were structured around the question, "What now regulates primary production and resulting plankton trophic dynamics in this region?" The initial phase of the project produced three general objectives:

1. Determine the principal factors controlling the early events in plankton production in the eastern Mediterranean.

2. Correlate the distribution of the primary (phytoplankton) and secondary (zooplankton) producers to local fisheries in both temporal and spatial domains.

3. Select the data from the coastal zone-color scanner on the NIMBUS-7 Satellite to determine the widths and structural features of the coastal areas as they pertain to total phytoplankton pigment concentrations.

Research findings made it clear that the project was working in an area of very low overall biological productivity. The investigations also showed the very different conditions existing in the near shore water mass and in the offshore (greater than 100 fathoms) areas. Chlorophyll measurements formed the backbone of the observational aspects of the project; samples were obtained from shipboard and through the use of the satellite-based coastal zone color scanner.

An important finding by the Egyptian scientists was that the overwhelming contribution to the chlorophyll-standing crop and the primary productivity of the waters was from nanoplankton, the smallest of the creatures (less than 20 micrometers in diameter).

Another important finding related to the widely differing species composition of the diatoms and dinoflagellates encountered during cruises at different times of the year. Of the five most abundant species of dinoflagellates, only one was recorded in the samples of both summer and winter cruises.

Finally, the early findings of this project were that the near shore and offshore water masses represent almost entirely separate ecosystems. As the various projects in the program matured over the decade, it became evident that the circulation of the eastern Mediterranean was considerably more complex and sophisticated than had been observed in earlier cruises.

From that jumping-off point in the research project, the next goals were as follows:

1. To define the important zooplankton and larval fish species.

2. To determine their associated spatial and temporal distribution in relation to phytoplankton and biomass and primary productivity.

These associations and distributions, largely unknown in both horizontal and vertical terms for the eastern Mediterranean, required immediate attention.

From the above, these crystallized the objectives of mapping seasonal distribution of the major groups of the various fish plankton larvae and obtaining data on their nutrition rates, and finally, synthesizing all the collected data to outline a sound basis for future fishery policy. This would also clarify future research goals for both Egypt and Israel in biological oceanography and fishery science.

This project took place between 1980 and 1985. Findings were represented as a series of tables showing distribution of larvae and fishstocks by area and by time of year. They indicated overall that the eastern Mediterranean is not one of the world's better fishing groups. This, of course, militated strongly for the countries to redirect their efforts more toward fish *farming* than fishing in the wild.

Over the next several years, scientists in the three participating countries digested the data and produced a large number of reports. In the process it became evident that the data and derived knowledge would be sufficient to permit a more sophisticated project relating to the distribution and abundance of commercially important fish, as well as the factors governing their production.

Accordingly, the group proposed a second phase of the project dealing with the Trophodynamics of the Southeastern Mediterranean, with Special Reference to Commercially Important Fishes. This project's objectives included the following:

1. Assess the standing stocks of commercially important fish species.
2. Determine production rates of these fish stocks.
3. Evaluate the potential for increasing fish harvest.
4. Search for unexploited stocks of pelagic species that might support an offshore fishery.

It was perceived that mutual cooperation in joint research efforts and scientific exchange between participants from Egypt and Israel would result in a sound scheme for optimal utilization of the living marine resources of the region.

This phase of the project is still ongoing. Unfortunately, the recent career of this particular project is distinctly emblematic of the ancient saying "for want of the nail...the kingdom was lost." A special, state-of-the-art echosounder was needed to conduct this project. The scientists in the three cooperating countries agreed that the only competent and reliable apparatus was produced by the Norwegian company, SIMRAD. Unfortunately, their pleas notwithstanding, they were ordered by the sponsoring government agency to "buy American," and a dismal series of failures of the equipment at sea caused the loss of at least a year and a half, and about \$100,000 worth of equipment and time. Although the project started in 1992, the equipment did not function properly until August of 1994, following a number of overhauls by the manufacturer.

By this time, the Egyptians were experiencing grave difficulties in acquiring a competent vessel for the field phases of the project, which caused serious gaps in overall accomplishment. On the other hand, their misfortune significantly increased their motivation to participate on the Israeli research vessel, thus leading to more intensive collaboration between the two countries. The Egyptians finally mounted cruises very late in 1994. During all of the cruises, physical, chemical, and biological parameters were studied, as had been done in the earlier phases of the project. This time, however, they were coupled with successful deployment of the hydroacoustic system.

Shoreline Erosion

The second major project concerned studies and development of a predictive model for shoreline changes along the Nile delta and neighboring regions.

This project involved collaboration among the University of California, San Diego (Scripps Institution of Oceanography's Center for Coastal Studies); the University of Alexandria Faculty of Engineering, in Egypt; the Egyptian Institute of Coastal Protection; and the National Institute of Oceanographic and Limnological Research in Haifa, Israel.

The fundamental issue underpinning this project also has its origin in the Aswan Dam. Millions of years ago, Egypt's shoreline was determined by equilibrium between the Nile River (which supplies) and the Mediterranean Sea (which takes). The Aswan Dam, by retaining approximately 160 million tons of sediment per year, has caused a radical shift in the equilibrium, with the result that the delta and shoreline have undergone severe erosion during this century. Mitigation of the effects of erosion and further development along this important coastal zone require an understanding of the forcing functions that drive sediment transport and coastal processes within the cell. To that purpose, a trilateral research program (as reported above) was formed with the ultimate objective of developing a predictive model for shoreline change as an essential step in applying the research findings to the practical aspects of coastal zone planning in that area. While the Egyptian coastline was immediately affected, there appeared to be no doubt in the minds of the Israeli scientists and engineers that the effect would eventually be felt on Israel's coast as well.

The erosion first became evident near the turn of the century, with construction of the low Aswan Dam, but the damage became serious in the 1960s upon completion of the high dam. An example of the rate of erosion, in this particular case of the Rosetta promontory, between 1900 and 1990, is shown in Figure 7.

For the purposes of the project, the Scripps Institution of Oceanography developed a highly sophisticated, automated recording sensor for measurements of winds, waves, etc. The instrument, known as the CASS recorder, was deployed at Abu Quir and Ras el-bar in Egypt, and Ashkelon and Haifa, in Israel, as shown in Figure 8. These stations measured wave heights, frequencies, and direction, thus allowing computations of wave energy flux in the nearshore zone. From this, the potential for longshore transport of sand was evaluated. In addition, beach profiling (mostly in Egypt) and coastal air photography (mostly in Israel) were carried out in order to monitor coastal changes caused either by natural processes or by engineering activities in the coastal zone. Placement of the stations is shown in Figure 8.

Results obtained during the first six years of the project enabled a follow-on phase to formulate a numerical model which, following proper field verification, will ultimately enable forecasting of coastal changes due to natural processes or manmade interventions in the shore zone. The input to the model was the data bank of wave, wind, current, and seabottom bathymetry measurements collected during the previous phase of the project.

Stated in practical terms, the participating scientists wished to determine the probable longevity of structures planned for installation at or near the shore, and efficacy of structures intended to reduce or halt erosion.

In the measurement process, the team reinforced the "new" appearance of eastern Mediterranean circulation by observing how water and sediment transport were effected by "mini-gyres" whose presence has only recently been recognized. Earlier, the appearance of the Mediterranean was a general counterclockwise circulation at the surface and a clockwise circulation below. This picture is now recognized, from the more detailed data recently obtained, to be vastly oversimplified. The circulation pattern is now understood to be composed of many small eddies or gyres, both clockwise and counterclockwise.

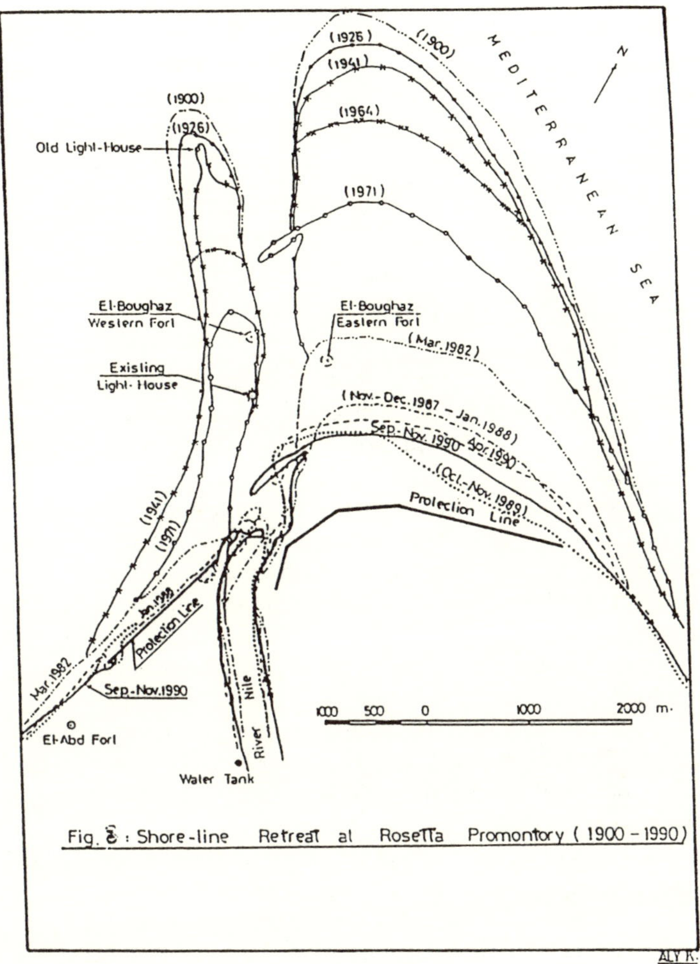

Figure 7. Shoreline retreat at Rosetta Promontory.

By now, the basic analysis framework for the shoreline model has been established. The model structure has been outlined. The required input data for the model have been determined and assessed. The Israeli and Egyptian participants continue to collect wave data at the four stations. Field experiments are being planned to accurately test the model. Thus far, results of the model are qualitatively in good agreement with observed patterns of erosion and accretion.

The social achievements of this project may well rank with the engineering. This was the first project in which publications were co-authored by Israelis and Egyptians. Further, the Egyptian principal investigator, Dr. Ahmed Khafagi, was the first Egyptian member of the program to visit Israel, and, in fact, was given a consultantship by the Israeli government in connection with silting problems along Tel Aviv beaches.

Aquaculture/Mariculture

Although the terms "aquaculture" and "mariculture" are often used interchangeably, such usage is incorrect. "Aquaculture" refers to fish farming in all aquatic media, while "mariculture" refers only to fish farming in sea water.

Although all of the projects in the marine program were selected for their utilitarian characteristics, probably the most important necessarily relate to food. This, in turn, derives from the position of water as pivotal to peace in the Middle East. As stated in Chapter 1, the reasoning process flows as follows:

Eighty percent of the potable water in the Middle East is used for agriculture. A 10 percent decrease in this usage would permit a greater than 20 percent increase in the amount available for civilian and industrial purposes. The incremental loss in food resources can clearly be made up in consumption of fish, but it must come from farming rather than fishing in the wild.

The cooperative research program has involved both seawater and brackish water owing to the presence of brackish water ponds in both countries. In Israel, these ponds lie near the ocean and are fed by the very few small rivers in Israel. In Egypt, they are far more prominent, including lakes Manzala, Burullous, Etku, and Maryut, which are essentially Nile drainage basins. Since both countries have almost unlimited access to the Mediterranean, however, seawater fish farming offers attractive possibilities.

Although subjects of study have included the gilt-head sea bream, tilapia, and sea bass, more effort has probably been exerted on the grey mullet than any other species. This is because sea mullet breed prolifically,

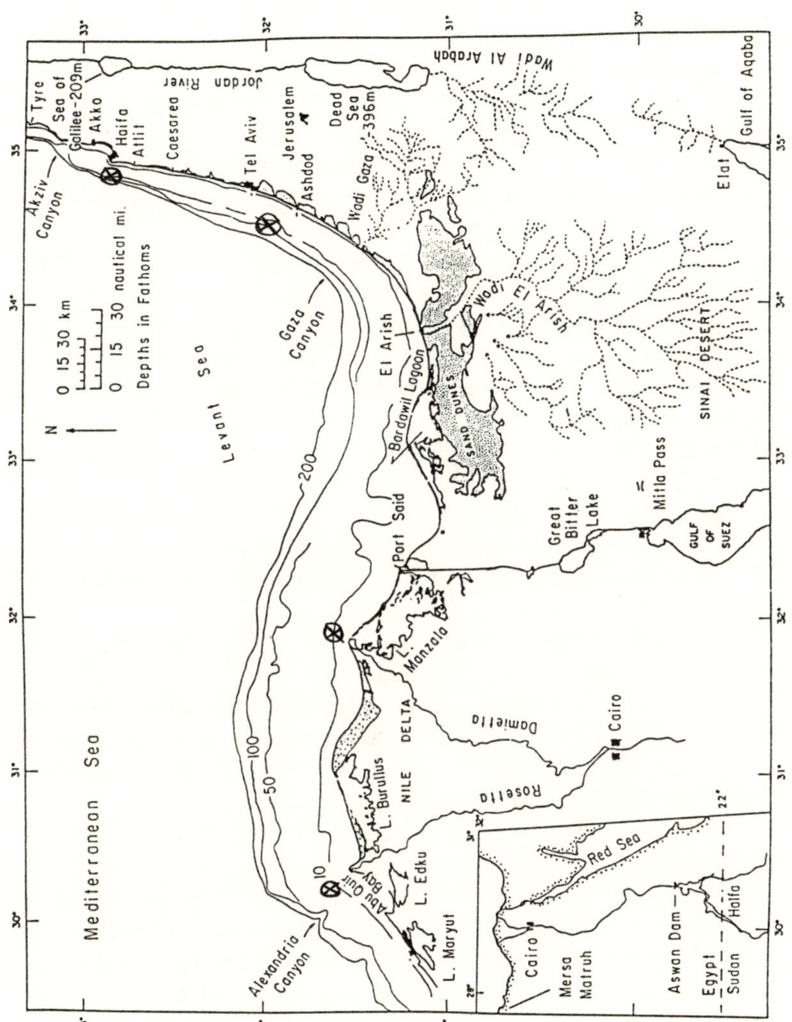

Figure 8. Placement of wave recording stations.

grow rapidly and easily, and provide an attractive food resource for residents in all of the Middle East countries. In many respects, mullet is the "third world fish."

The mullet is also an attractive candidate for farming in both seawater and brackish water for the following reasons:
1. It thrives in a wide range of salinities, from seawater to freshwater.
2. It grows fast and is amenable to a simple diet, which does not have to contain high levels of expensive protein.
3. It grows well on the natural food available in its environment. Detritus, algae, and small benthic organisms are as good a feed for the grey mullet as dry pelleted feed.

The principle objectives of the mullet culture projects are to increase knowledge and understanding of the fish's reproductive processes, with emphasis on controlling these processes and inducing the fish to accelerate the breeding process through administration of hormones and other procedures.

Objectives include the following:
1. Study of the reproductive cycle through year-round measurement of energy transfer into the muscle, skin, and various tissues of the fish.
2. Establishment of a well-acclimated brood stock suitable for inducement of artificial spawning.
3. Inducement of spawning through injection of various hormones, followed by incubating the artificially fertilized eggs through hatching, nursing, and feeding the hatchlings with cultured plankton until the fry (growing up) stage.

The first two objectives were readily and successfully accomplished.

In Israel, the fingerlings are reared in fresh or brackish water under polyculture conditions, together with common carp, grass carp, silver carp, and tilapia. Grey mullet commands the highest price on the local market. However, its farming is based exclusively on fry, caught around river runoffs. In the past, numbers of fry collected were sufficient to support a moderate-sized farming operation. In recent years, pollution of the rivers and overfishing have dramatically reduced the number of fry collected, and the aquaculture industry is suffering from underproduction of this important species. In Egypt, the same conditions prevail. The grey mullet is the most prestigious fish, and the fry catch situation is similar to that of Israel.

For these reasons, it is crucial that a technology facilitating production of grey mullet fingerlings be developed and established.

The hormonal pathway has been fairly well established, enabling the scientists in both countries (mainly in Egypt, however) to manipulate the maturation processes through environmental and further hormonal treatments.

Unfortunately, the mullet, in common with many marine fishes targeted for mariculture, usually fails to spawn spontaneously in captivity. The Israelis have succeeded in spawning some adult mullets at this point in time.

One problem the Israelis encountered was that for reasons not understood, the grey mullet males reached spermiation a few weeks prior to the females' readiness to spawn, and by the time the females reached the stage of spawning ability, in early January, the males were already spent. The hormonal therapy given by the Israelis caused the males to produce sperm again, and spawning was then induced using various hormonal implants.

Another fish that is highly prized, particularly in the Mediterranean, is the sea bass. Most of the work on this species has revolved about creation and development of an optimum feed that will result in the best growth for the lowest price. The growth of sea bass on lipid sources indicates a requirement for what is called the "N-3 family" of fatty acids for better growth. Changes in their body fatty acid composition have indicated the fishes' ability to synthesize the other intermediate acids in the pathway to higher growth. Primarily in Israel, intensive studies have been and continue to be carried out on the degree to which the sea bass can synthesize its own acids for optimum growth.

In the process, six grow-out rations were tested for their effect on the growth of sea bass through a limited size range of up to 35–45 grams. Three of the better performing rations were subsequently tested on larger fish and appeared to be providing good growth and survival.

Although some work is being initiated in Egypt on the sea bream, most of it has been carried out for two decades in Israel, at the National Mariculture Center in Eilat. An arrangement has been forged with five kibbutzim (resident communities) whereby the National Mariculture Center performs strongly application-oriented research on these fish to develop the entire growth cycle, and the kibbutzim market the fish all over Europe.

It took nearly a decade for the Israelis to solve the complete cycle and to encourage the bream to spawn in captivity, but that finally has been accomplished. For the past half decade, the Israelis have been receiving highly significant revenue from markets primarily in Italy and France, where the fish are marketed as Denise or Dorad.

Unfortunately for the Middle Easterners, mariculture, which had been a subordinate industry in Europe until about ten years ago, has recently begun to blossom as conventional food sources have become prohibitively expensive. Literally hundreds of mariculture plants have sprung up in Turkey, Greece, Yugoslavia, and Italy, and on France's and Spain's Mediterranean coasts, with the result that market prices for sea bass, trout, and bream-the primary targets of fish farms—have sharply declined in the last half decade. This is good news for society and bad news for the farmers. Accordingly, an all-European conference took place in Verona in October 1995 to explore possibilities of controlling these important markets.

In Egypt, and to a slightly lesser extent in Israel, tilapia contribute the highest production figures among the species commonly cultured in fish farms. Most of the research conducted in both countries has centered about hybridization of tilapia for faster growth rates and other qualities. The Egyptians have concentrated their efforts on the tilapia nilotica (from the Nile River and outflow) and the aurea, common to both countries. The Israelis have worked on the same species and also on the galilaeus, commonly known in the United States as St. Peter's fish. They have cross-bred these species and also a red tilapia species of Taiwanese origin.

A problem peculiar to tilapia is that they grow so fast that at any given point in time, the smaller fish so outnumber the larger, more mature fish in pond, that they acquire most of the food, with a consequent reduction in larger, marketable fish. Commonly, the Israelis prefer a 250-gram fish for broiling, and the Egyptians a 125-gram fish for pan frying. For this reason, one of the objectives of the product was production of a monosex tilapia, which would breed either slowly or not at all. The Egyptians have concentrated on attempting to produce an all-male tilapia in the spawning process. An enormous amount of data has been collected on production rates of fingerlings, growth rates of the young fish, disease resistance, and flavor from four types of cross-breeding. At one point, a strain was introduced from the Ivory Coast as well. The Egyptians succeeded in producing a breeding system resulting in between 65 and 85 percent males, with an average of 79 percent. Later they attained figures between 81 and 83 percent.

The cross-breeding projects have produced male hybrid fingerlings that grow faster than any of the parent species, and can attain Egyptian market size in about four months from birth! The Israelis, in addition to collaborating with the Egyptians, experimented with cheaper feeds, including dry poultry manure and 25 percent protein feed pellets (mainly from fish).

To date, the most outstanding phenomenon in the data appears to be the large variation in survival rates, as shown in a number of reports and tables produced by the Israelis and Egyptians. This project is a good example of sustainability in that scientists and engineers in both countries continue the work, although funding ceased approximately three years ago. It is also a good example of the trend from parallel bilateral affiliations, through trilateral affiliations, to a Mideastern bilateral, in that the two countries are now dealing directly with each other without American participation. It is also an area where Jordanian participation is imminent.

Reiterating previous comments, the principal attraction of mariculture is its ability to produce food without use of desperately needed potable water. There are two fundamental approaches to mariculture:

1. Seawater ponds limited to the ocean by canals.
2. Ocean culture per se using cages and nets.

The advantage of saltwater pond culture is control. Without proper control, fish farming's Achilles heel is its deleterious effect on the environment, resulting primarily from fish feces. In ponds, environmental preservation is accomplished through polyculture, where fish droppings are utilized by detritus feeders, such as shellfish. Once equilibrium is attained, the farm's effluent may be cleaner than the original intake. The disadvantage is one of logistics. Ponds and canals must be dug. This is expensive; moreover, adequate water circulation must be ensured, whatever the cost.

The advantage of open sea culture is that the "farm" already exists and simply awaits usage. Further, nature provides a degree of water circulation, or flushing. Disadvantages are as follows:

1. The need for competent structural engineering to protect the cages from waves and storms. In practice, the cases are semi-submerged or part of an elevator system that lowers them below wave action during storms.
2. Loss of environmental control. Seawater cages or nets are normally fixed on site. In spite of the natural circulation in the ocean, therefore, fecal droppings tend to concentrate on the ocean

bottom, allowing eutrophication (i.e., weed proliferation), which is an undesirable environmental development.

Regardless of the species or site selection, the fundamental approach is the same: assessment in depth of every factor involved in the culture process. This is illustrated in Figure 9.

Lake Management

While the physical environments involved in the preceding research projects have been more or less identical between Israel and Egypt and have represented a continuum, rather than a geographic discontinuance between the two countries, the lake management project has featured rather different research environments.

As noted previously, several lakes in Egypt have been formed by the Nile distributaries: Manzala, Burrulous, Etku, and Maryut. On the other hand, Israel has but one sizable lake, the Sea of Galilea, or Lake Kinneret (depending on who is describing it). Nonetheless, there is enough fundamental similarity between the two environments to attract excellent scientific cooperation and exchange among the Egyptian, Israeli, and American scientists. In another example of progress from parallel bilateral, though trilateral, to Mideastern bilateral, American participation was phased out in 1986.

Originally, the project focused on two intensively exploited lakes, Manzala in Egypt, and Kinneret in Israel. More recently, Egyptian emphasis has transferred to Lake Burrulous because of its greater importance to the fishing industry.

The major objectives of this project are as follows:
1. To assess the distribution of biomass;
2. To analyze the energy flow pathways from phytoplankton through zooplankton, into the commercial fish species;
3. To evaluate the impact of major fishery techniques on the fish community structure; and
4. To develop management recommendations.

The Israelis had to focus somewhat more heavily on the biological food chain owing to the tendency of Lake Kinneret to eutrophy (a process in which weeds, forming at the bottom of a lake, tend to grow out of control and eventually take over the lake and effectively suffocate it). The Egyptians, on the other hand, had to contend with massive pollution problems.

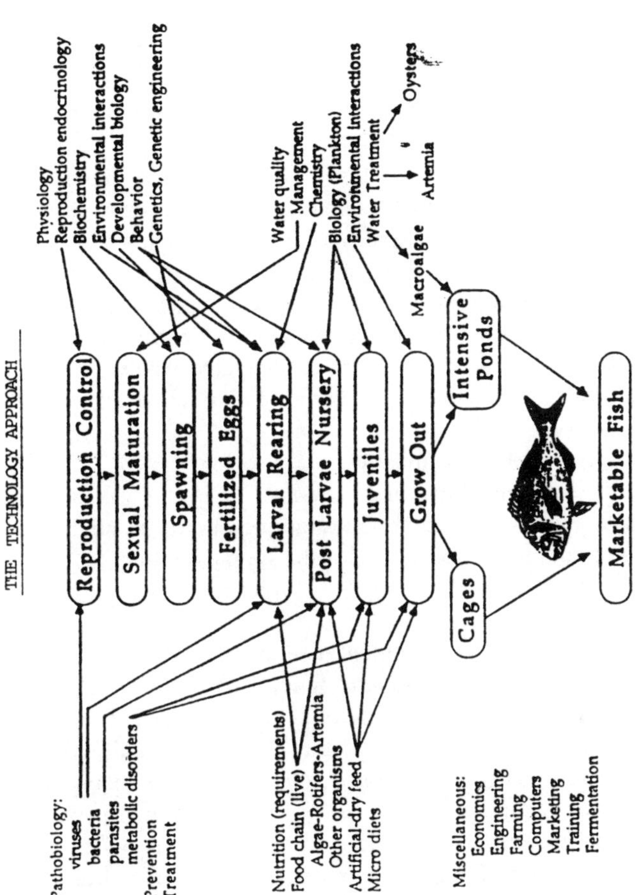

Figure 9. Schematic description of the interdisciplinary nature of mariculture and the interactions among these disciplines.

In recent years however, macrophyte (weed) populations have increased in Egypt's Lake Manzala. Observations have indicated that they occur as dense mats estimated to cover 30 to 50 percent of the lake basin in some seasons. Although in some cases dense weed populations impede commercial fishing operations, at the same time they contribute to fish recruitment by serving as nursery and spawning areas (habitats) and by producing food resources. The Egyptians believe changes in the macrophyte populations are caused by declines in salinity levels in the lakes, since the weeds seem to do better in fresh water. Thus the Egyptians have been actively measuring the distribution of biomass and investigating the relationship between these masses and salinities, using field surveys backed up by remote-sensing techniques.

Lake Kinneret provides two-thirds of Israel's drinking water. Its sensitivity can thus only be remotely imagined by Americans. It receives water mostly from the Jordan River and is the only natural freshwater lake in Israel. The cooperative program provided the first experimental investigations of fish feeding selectivities and their impacts on the plankton communities of the lake were reported as a major scientific achievement. Other major findings include indications of competition between the most valuable commercial fishery, the St. Peter's fish (Galilaeus), and other stocked fishes.

Thus, major Israeli goals include the following:

1. Studies of competitive interactions;
2. Assessment of plankton community response to predation by major competing species that subsist on plankton;
3. Evaluation of major fishery techniques on fish community structures;
4. Development of management recommendations.

The Israelis also wish to extend laboratory analyses of feeding behavior, selectivity, and metabolism to include other important species of fish for comparison with the St. Peter's fish. Incidentally, the large sardine population in the lake is considered not only as noncontributing to the food value of the lake, but as a "trash" fish, which is extensive enough to cause problems, but insufficiently extensive to provide solutions (such as fertilizer, fish feed, etc.). In other words, the sardines, not considered to be edible, compete for food with the commercial species. On the other hand, the population is not dense enough to market as pet food. Thus the Israelis burn them, when caught!

Foreign species are being introduced with extreme caution. Another goal has been testing the results of laboratory feeding and metabolism experiments in large outdoor tanks and enclosures in the lake itself. The Israelis have examined interaction effects between plankton and seven species of fish.

The use of sonar and other experimental hydroacoustic systems has enabled the determination of fish distribution and selection of optimal fishing gear and techniques. In the process, the Israelis have developed a highly sophisticated technique for three-dimensional depiction of fish stocks in the lake over space and time.

At this point in time, studies are still ongoing, with considerable interaction between the Israeli and Egyptian scientists. It is one of the best examples of equal contribution, and therefore a source of pride to all of the participating scientists. The studies have produced innumerable reports, which in Israel have already resulted in regulatory changes, with particular reference to fishing permits. In Egypt, the results have been brought to the attention of officials who are considering the same thing, as well as stricter pollution regulations. Specifically, the Israeli scientists have communicated to the National Department of Fisheries the need to increase the stocking rate of the Galilaeus and to reduce the population of "lavnun" (the Lake Kinneret sardine). Both recommendations are apparently in process of implementation at this time. Interactions at all levels of the biological food chain have been noted in extreme detail. This is especially valuable during particularly wet or particularly dry seasons, when the level of the lake varies and has to be controlled with caution.

The Israelis reported a dramatic increase in the number of fish starting in mid-1992, which leveled off in 1993, followed by a further increase in the stock of the sardine in 1994. They attribute the increase, at least in part, to the rise in the lake levels, which made a number of additional potential spawning sites available during the 1991–92 spawning season.

The Israeli and Egyptian scientists were using the same advanced hydroacoustic gear that proved catastrophic in the case of the trophodynamics project. Fortunately, this apparatus was less critical to the success of the total project than to the trophodynamics project.

In Egypt, the project has enabled scientists to make far more detailed measurements than at any time in history. This has led to much more complete understanding of the food chains in all of the lakes and their interrelationships.

It has further allowed the Egyptians to transfer attention to Lake Qarun, approximately 60 miles (100 km) south of Cairo. This lake is different from those previously cited in that it is not a Nile drainage basin. It was once the largest oasis in the Sahara, but owing to misuse, salinity has increased to a level almost equal to that of the Mediterranean Sea itself. The result has been a change from freshwater to saltwater species.

Recent activities have centered on this lake, including intensive monthly surveys. In each trip to the lake, samples for physical, chemical, and biological parameters of the lake water and sediment were collected from 24 stations in both the lake itself and its two main drains. Also, experiments are in progress to monitor fish populations, catch composition, and reproduction of the native as well as the planted fish (including mullet). Pollution of the lake has come under considerable examination as well. Exactly as in the case of Lake Kinneret, interrelationships between the phytoplankton and zooplankton have been measured, as well as their ability to provide food to the various commercial species.

In summary, in the process of transferring attention to Lake Qarun, the Egyptians have performed a heroic series of experiments relating to the most minute observations and determinations of fish growth, disease probability, and relationship of all species to water clarity. Ultimately, as a result of these observations, the productivity of the lake is expected to approximately double.

Seafood Safety

The next project, Seafood Safety, began conventionally but underwent a curious metamorphosis. It started early in the life of the program (1985) as "Seafood Toxins," intended as a collaboration between Egypt's National Research Centre and Israel's Institute for Oceanographic and Limnological Research. Emblematic of the complexities encountered throughout this program, the Egyptian partner, Dr. Khayria Naguib, brilliant director of the Centre's Mycology Department, developed an antipathy to traveling in Israel and working with Israelis. As nearly as could be determined, her attitude stemmed from fear of Palestinian retaliation.

Thus, while the planned division of effort assigned organic contaminant study to the Egyptians and heavy metal analysis to the Israelis, the Egyptians suddenly announced discovery of a local laboratory capable of performing the heavy metal determinations. This action, however, abrogated the program's charter and the project's mission. Finally, total responsibility for an international symposium on Seafood Toxins, which was integral to the project proposal, was assumed by the Egyptians. They excluded the Israelis. AID support funds were immediately withdrawn by the author, as program coordinator.

Paradoxically, at the end of the project, the Egyptians published the most heroically comprehensive report of any project in the program's history.[1] The Israelis published separately.

While failing to adhere to either the letter or spirit of the program, the projects did produce useful information, principally that organochlorine pesticides are present in fish caught in Egypt, although at very low concentrations and well within the safety limits prescribed by the U.S. Food and Drug Administration. Although the use of DDT was prohibited in Egypt in the early 1960s, accumulation was found to be the highest of all pesticide residues. Finally, it was determined that no single pesticide predominates in any of Egypt's lakes (i.e., Nile drainage basins).

Significantly, the 36 references cited in the Egyptian report failed to include any Israeli publications.

Three years later (in 1992) the project was essentially revivified under a new name, Seafood Safety, and under new management, a closely cooperative effort among the following:

1. The Department of Environmental and Industrial Health, The University of Michigan, USA.
2. The Environmental Health Laboratory, Division of Environmental Sciences, Hebrew University of Jerusalem, Israel.
3. The National Institute of Oceanography and Fisheries, Cairo University, Egypt.
4. Ain Shams University, Egypt.

The project in its new incarnation aimed to develop health and safety guidelines to protect seafood from contamination. These guidelines are intended to serve as the basis for the development of regulations in the Middle East to assure consumers that the seafood products they purchase meet accepted minimum standards for safety.

The project's stated goals included assessment of public health and safety practices used in the production, marketing, and consumption of seafood in Egypt and Israel; promotion of awareness of the health risk of seafood contaminants; and development of guidelines for improvement of seafood production and marketing. The institutions involved sought to examine the feasibility of various options to minimize risks of seafood-borne illness with emphasis on fish decontamination procedures. Thus, although encompassing ambitious laboratory objectives, the project was aimed considerably farther than its predecessor, i.e., to penetrate the public domain. To date, participants have completed the planned investigations on schedule, including training, developing a data bank for both chemical and microbial contaminants, and reviewing current literature regarding chemical and microbial contamination of seafood and its public health safety implications. Between October 1, 1993, and September 30, 1994, researchers in Egypt and Israel completed several experiments to investigate fish decontamination and depuration rates and to assess microbial and chemical contamination in fish from various sites in Egypt.

Examination of fish from the Aswan area showed a prevalence of parasitic infections, but this value was low relative to values observed in the north of Egypt. Bacteriological examination revealed relatively low levels of bacteria and coliform, indicating that pollution with bacteria was minimal. Bacteria were isolated from the skin, and tests did not detect these bacteria in the muscles.

Chemical examination focused on the uptake, accumulation, and elimination of the insecticide fenitrothion, various metals, proteins, lipids, and polycyclic aromatic hydrocarbons (PAHS). Researchers determined that the accumulation of fenitrothion was greater for larger fish. Depuration results of fish contaminated with the insecticide showed that concentrations declined gradually, with no significant difference between large and small fish at the end of the 15-day elimination period.

Project scientists measured levels of cadmium, lead, copper, and zinc in the gills, liver, and muscles of fish collected from several sites in Egypt. A detailed experiment on the uptake and elimination of cadmium illustrates its capacity to bioaccumulate, especially in gill tissues. Uptake of cadmium was rapid, while elimination from the tissue proceeded rather slowly. PAH experiments showed site-specific differences in fish concentration levels. Total hydrocarbons were highest in fish samples collected from the north, in the Port Said area. This is most likely due to the heavy sea traffic. Total protein content of fish muscle showed nonsignificant variation at different sites.

A study took place to determine the effectiveness of pathogen depuration from fish. It examined the effectiveness of changing the water in holding tanks to reduce the level of microorganisms in various fish tissues. Results of the study indicated that faster decontamination of fish is achieved by repeatedly changing the water in the holding tanks.

Risk analyses highlighted mercury and cadmium as potential problems among the metals examined.

Circulation of the Levantine Basin

This project, which in some ways should have been the most far-reaching of all the projects (and may yet be, someday) failed to achieve its goals, mainly because of logistics failures.

The title itself is misleading in that the aim was to correlate energy exchange between ocean and atmosphere with the "storm effect" (i.e., rain probabilities) over ensuing seasons. The work was collaborative among the Alexandria branch of Egypt's National Institute of Oceanography and Fisheries, the Institute of Oceanography and Limnology in Haifa, and Princeton University.

A model of the entire Mediterranean Basin was created and used to study the influence of different surface forcing on the circulation. For instance, when simulating the average or climatological circulation of the sea, it is often sufficient to use climatological surface forcing fields including wind force and direction, sea surface heights, fresh water influx, etc. There are, however, many aspects of circulation that depend on the day-to-day variations in air/sea interactions. The concern of the participating scientists related mainly to failure of previous studies to pay attention to synoptic variability in favor of the climatological (i.e., average) features of the Mediterranean Sea.

In order to prepare almost daily presentations of surface heights and wind stress fields, the Israelis obtained the twice daily analyses from the European Center for Medium Range Weather Forecast. They converted these data into surface flux fields and then interpolated the data on the mandatory levels to obtain surface pressure as well as the wind complements, temperature, and specific humidity at 10 meters above the surface (the standard level used for bulk computation). Since additional needed parameters, i.e., sea surface temperature and total cloud cover, were not furnished by the European Center, they used the monthly mean climatological fields for sea surface temperature and derived the cloud cover from an empirical relationship as a function of relative humidity and pressure.

Solar radiation values were determined from daily clear sky values at the Smithsonian meteorological tables. Back radiation cooling of the surface was obtained from calculations involving sea surface temperature, atmospheric temperature, humidity, and cloud cover.

The resulting general synoptic situation appeared to consist of a low pressure system over the eastern Mediterranean basin and strong northerly winds over the western Mediterranean. The researchers also noticed the sharp radiant cloud cover between the low pressure and the dry air over northern Egypt.

All of these data and computations were compiled to feed into the "Princeton Ocean Model" developed by Blumberg and Miller in 1987.[2]

This approach enabled a number of experiments:

1. The model was forced with the monthly wind stress average while the surface temperature and salinity were fixed to be equal to the annual averages in order to simulate perpetual annual average conditions.

2. Monthly wind stress averages, monthly surface energy influx, and surface salinity flux, which is constant in time and space, were obtained by prescribing through the model an evaporative fresh water flux of one meter per year, corresponding to that estimated for the Mediterranean Sea in 1979.

3. The wind stress and surface energy forcings continued in the second experiment, but the monthly averaged spatially varying surface salinity flux was calculated and applied, and an annually averaged fresh water input was introduced.

The integration times were five years for the first two experiments and six years for the third experiment.

The Egyptian groups studied the tidal motion of the Mediterranean Sea as one of the factors controlling the circulation. In order to achieve this goal, a mathematical model was selected and developed and several experiments were performed. The study was carried out in steps. The first experiment was set to test the mathematical model considering two closed rectangular basins of constant depth connected by a two-degree wide opening. Subsequent experiments idealized the Mediterranean as a singular rectangular basin and then as an I-shaped basin with constant depths of 500 and 1,500 meters, respectively.

The results of the numerical simulations of the entire Mediterranean Basin indicate that the model is able to reproduce the main features of Mediterranean Sea circulation. Using the model, the scientists can now describe surface circulations in any given part of the eastern Mediterranean plus their seasonal variabilities. They can study at close quarters cyclonic gyre in the Roads Basin and (in summertime) an anti-cyclonic gyre close to the Egyptian coast. Utilizing these tools, the scientists were able to produce tables of circulation at a number of ocean depths as well as temperature and salinity fields for those same depths.

An important factor in the program related to capacity building in Egypt. Dr. Ibrahim Maiyza, from Alexandria, spent considerable time in Princeton to familiarize himself with the model and perform several three-dimensional experiments. Dr. Steven Brenner from Haifa also visited Princeton several times, working with both the Princeton scientists and Dr. Maiyza.

While from a purely scientific viewpoint the above-mentioned results may have justified the project, it did fall short of its goals. As is evident from the above discussion, execution of the project depended largely on use of highly sophisticated computers. The computers in Haifa and Princeton matched very well. At the start of the project, however, the Egyptians possessed no such apparatus. Accordingly, they asked the program coordinator (the author) to purchase compatible equipment, specifying the characteristics and source of the computer system.

AID, however, was under legal obligation to utilize competitive bidding. The series of events culminating in acquisition of the appropriate gear occupied 19 months of the 36-month project. This series included drawing up specifications for the equipment; circulating the specifications for the request for bid; allowing appropriate time for digestion and turnaround in the bidding process; conducting a comparative analysis of the bids; awarding the contract; assembling the computer system; transporting the equipment to Alexandria; and setting it up at the institute's Alexandria laboratory. Princeton and Haifa were using a Sun Radio Systems Corporation system uniquely suited to the project. Accordingly, it was argued that sole source procurement would be justified. The argument was unsuccessful. Sun Radio Systems eventually did win the bid and assembled the equipment, but when it arrived in Alexandria it was found that several wrong parts had been incorporated into the system and the process had to start all over again. Description of the towering frustrations experienced by all concerned is beyond the scope of this document.

Ultimately, the Israelis entered into separate negotiations with the U.S. National Oceanic and Atmospheric Administration for this work, but the two Middle Eastern countries and Princeton University retained interest in continuing the project. They were later joined in prospect by Brown University and the Mediterranean Research Center at Erice, Italy.

An "off-the-wall" but intriguing concept for future speculation concerns the possibility that if the correlation between ocean-atmosphere energy interchange can be clearly correlated with later rainfall enabling effective forecasting, then someday rainfall might actually be increased by lowering the sea surface temperature of the southeast Mediterranean by as little as one degree! (Techniques for achieving this result have already been suggested but are not relevant to this discussion.)

Notes

1. Naguib, Khayria Mahmood, Mohamed Mahmood Naguib, and Mohamed N.E.I. Gomaa, "Chemical Contaminants of Egyptian Seafoods," Egyptian National Research Centre, Cairo, 1993.
2. Blumberg, A.F., and G.L. Miller. Description of a Three Dimensional Coastal Ocean Circulation Model. In N.S. Heaps, ed., *Coastal Estuarine Science,* Vol. 4, pp. 1–16, Academic Press, London, 1987.

4. Analysis of the Program

Introduction

The question of what effect, if any, the program has had on reducing tensions in the Middle East must inevitably be asked. While it is always difficult, if not impossible, to remain completely objective in analyzing one's own work, in this case the author is aided by four previous evaluations, conducted by external teams of experts recruited and assigned by the U.S. Agency for International Development. Accordingly, full use will be made of these evaluations, quoting liberally and appending the complete reports to this document. The evaluations were conducted by the following individuals:

1. Drs. Herman Pollack and Clarence Idyll in 1983. Dr. Pollack was the previous science advisor to the secretary of state and had achieved an international reputation for his work in international science and technology. At the time of the evaluation, he was distinguished professor of international science and technology at the George Washington University. Dr. Idyll was chief of the division of fisheries at the University of Miami and internationally known for his many works in the fields of fisheries and aquaculture.

2. Drs. Charles Busch and Conrad Recksiek in 1986. Dr. Busch had achieved an outstanding reputation as a troubleshooter and consulting engineer in the field of international in aquaculture and was employed by AID on several previous occasions to restore failing projects. Dr. Recksiek was a professor of marine biology at the University of Rhode Island.

3. Ambassador C. William Kontos, Dr. William Reinke, and Dr. Quentin M. West in 1991 (under the aegis of the Devres Corporation under contract to AID). These gentlemen had many decades of experience in international politics and technology and had demonstrated outstanding capabilities to penetrate program facades to arrive at true values.

    4.   Drs. John Eriksen, Stephan Grilli, and Jean-Yves Mevel in 1993. Dr. Anderson was an economist who had participated in several AID evaluations previously and Drs. Grilli and Mevel, although inexperienced, were known as comers in their fields.

It is now necessary to return to the process of mandate. When the initial AID grant was awarded—and it should be remembered that this was the first of its kind, ever—the only formal guidance was legislative, in the original Waxman Amendment to the Foreign Assistance Act of 1977. As stated in that bill, the goal was to encourage Middle Eastern countries to work together, with Israel mandated as one of the partners.[1]

AID understood this very well at the time. During the first interview with then-acting administrator of the bureau, Joseph Wheeler, the author was counseled: "Remember, this isn't just another scientific project; the idea is to get all these people working together." Quite often, in those early days, the author was reminded by the AID officials, "Remember, Bob, this isn't the National Science Foundation!"[2]

Whether or not the program's managers succeeded, or how well they succeeded, at least the guidance was clear.

About mid-decade, however, the guidelines shifted perceptibly, as economic benefits became recognized as legitimate and desirable objectives. They assumed increasing importance in the program's evaluation structure as time went on. Since economic payoff could reasonably be identified with the goal of togetherness (as long as such payoffs were fairly equally issued), the technique was workable. Some of the projects were amenable to such analysis; others were not. AID cannot be faulted for its stance; after all, it had been grading projects by the number of calves born per year in Africa for several decades, ever since its establishment. It was a game with which it was familiar.

While mariculture is relatively amenable to such evaluative practice, other projects, such as general oceanography of the Mediterranean or primary productivity of the eastern Mediterranean, are less easily tracked. The attempt was made, nonetheless.

Then, in the late 1980s, the dictum appeared to shift once again, this time in the direction of the merit of the science itself. This philosophy occasioned some tremors in the teams already on site, especially those in each others' fields, so to speak. Does a highly scholarly investigation into the chemistry of the southeast Mediterranean really outrank the production of food fish? The answer appeared to be a qualified, "Well, not really, but...."

These shifts were undoubtedly merited from the perspective of the sponsoring agency, which was, after all, responsible for displaying annually a program deserving of continuing appropriations. Accordingly, the priorities perceived by the legislative branch of government became translated into those of the executive branch. Whether the perception was accurate or not was moot. Furthermore, these shifts transferred the balance of prominence in the program from managers to scientists (who may or may not be managers).

But now it is time to confront the question that is fundamental to this entire study: Has the program reduced tensions in the Middle East, and can it be expected to do so in the future? The answer is a definite "Maybe!"

External Evaluations: A History of Assessments of the MERC Marine Program

Fortunately for the purposes of this project, the MERC Program, especially the Marine Program, does not want for professional external evaluations. This is, in fact, a characteristic of the operating philosophy of the Agency for International Development, possibly because it has been so often maligned.

When the Cooperative Marine Technology Program for the Middle East was finally accepted by AID, its managers were advised that program evaluation would be a very important part of the program's routine. Because MERC was an entirely new enterprise from the AID perspective, however, guidelines were at best sparse, and we were asked to help "invent" them. At this point, one of the original partners, Dr. George E. Assousa, then a senior fellow at the Carnegie Institution of Washington, assumed leadership. He prepared the first program evaluation guide, which was submitted to AID for review and adopted.

Dr. Assousa's draft was partly based on existing AID doctrine, including "Program Evaluation in AID" (1976), "Project Evaluation Guidelines" (1974), and "Evaluation Handbook," second edition. Dr. Assousa referred to the AID "Logical Framework" (LOGFRAME) and later collaborated with Dr. Abel in the initial execution of the LOGFRAME pattern.

It is interesting to note that the initial evaluation of the MERC Program came from an external source unaffiliated with AID. During our first trip to Cairo, Dr. El-Sayed and I were given considerable assistance by U.S. Embassy personnel, especially in the science office. In 1979, the science counsellor to the ambassador was Dr. Addison Richmond, an engineer who was himself of North African origin. He became interested in our projects.

Shortly thereafter, Dr. Richmond was transferred to Washington for the Executive Seminar in National and International Affairs operated by the State Department's Foreign Service Institute. For his seminar thesis, Dr. Richmond wrote on "Normalization and Its Implications: The Development of Relations between Egypt and Israel Since 1977." Needless to say, this was one of the earliest essays on the subject, the Israel-Egypt accord having been signed in March 1979 and diplomatic relations established in January 1980.

It is interesting to note the partly prophetic nature of the thesis over the ensuing decade and a half; with full knowledge of what we were trying to accomplish, Dr. Richmond forecast participation by a number of institutions, none of which had actually started in the program, ignoring the IOLR and NIOF. Furthermore, he predicted a number of cooperative disciplines, again ignoring the marine technologies that actually started the program. "In Israel, planning for cooperation in various functional areas began soon after President Sadat's first visit. Workshops were held and working groups to develop and coordinate proposals established at several universities and institutions, notably the Tel Aviv and Hebrew Universities and the Technion. At other institutions various specific proposals in selected areas emerged. Interests focused particularly on research and development and cooperation in technical areas, including agriculture and land management, water resources, health, and energy." The projects that actually pioneered the program, i.e., mariculture, shoreline protection, and lakes management, however, were simply not considered at that time.

Richmond carefully analyzed the differences in approaches between the Israelis and Egyptians, accurately pointing out the personal risks— both financial and social—encountered by any Egyptians viewed as enhancing the interrelationships. At the end of his report, Richmond acknowledged that the Marine Program had grabbed an early lead and was the "largest of these projects." He named all of the projects in the program and judged the concept and initiation of the projects to be "promising both in their scientific content and in the collaboration established between Israeli and Egyptian scientists." Richmond's paper ends with a cogent and comprehensive plea for support for the MERC concept. His ending paragraph is particularly penetrating: "The United States can suggest and facilitate, especially in the early stages, but implementation, to be normal, must be the responsibility of Egypt and Israel."[3]

The first formal external evaluation of the MERC Marine Program was conducted by Drs. Herman Pollack and Clarence P. Idyll, both eminent in their communities and outstanding in their fields. Their evaluation was conducted and the report submitted to AID in March 1983.

The report began with an almost identical statement of Richmond's thesis that Israel appeared eager for rapid progress in cooperation, but Egypt, owing to its position in the Arab world, had to proceed with more caution. The report was laudatory, surprising even the project's practitioners. The team's opinion was that "Considering that cooperation in marine technology started from point zero and was confronted by understandable but nevertheless onerous Egyptian limitations as well as very formidable historic, political, and cultural obstacles, the Marine Technology Program has a surprisingly creditable record in establishing contacts between related specialists in Egypt and Israel. A basis for accelerated development of cooperation between the Egyptian and Israeli participants is now in place. Such development would occur if permitted or encouraged by the political and foreign policies of the two governments."

The team noted the absence of interaction and exchange among students, which has continued to plague the program, and they noted the failure of the senior Egyptians to visit Israel (which, of course, was overwhelmingly altered several years later). They concluded, "The program produced worthwhile science.... Predictably, some projects were more productive scientifically than others...." Their principal recommendations were for continued sponsorship of the program, more interaction among the scientists, progressive reduction of the Americans' roles, and that the bureaucracy of funding be diminished as much as possible to allow continuity of operations.[4]

The next evaluation was conducted in May 1985 by Drs. Charles Busch and Conrad Recksiek. Dr. Busch is an internationally acclaimed scientist-businessman who specializes in fish farming, and Dr. Recksiek is a marine biologist from the University of Rhode Island. As stated in their report, this team "found the situation to be much the same as when evaluated in Phase I.... [S]cience is generally outstanding and efforts towards normalization are doing as well as can be expected." The team noted three main problems:

1. Reluctance of Egyptians to travel to Israel.
2. Slow administrative procedures handicapping fund disbursement.
3. Absence of a unified logical framework.

Their evaluation of management for cooperation was favorable: "The Project Manager appears to be doing everything possible to achieve cooperation at all levels of the project including 'output'." "A high level of joint participation through professional exchange has been achieved." Finally, the team was enthusiastic about the ongoing work and results achieved in the various fish-farming experiments with both sea bream and tilapia.[5]

The next and probably most significant examination of the program was conducted by the Devres Corporation, under contract to AID, in January 1991. The report was submitted on February 6, 1991. This evaluation was particularly significant because it encompassed the entire MERC Program and was conducted at a high level of expertise. The team consisted of Ambassador C. William Kontos, Dr. William A. Reinke, and Dr. Quentin M. West, all able and highly experienced scientist-administrators. The task was conducted in stages: a week of briefing in Washington, two weeks in Egypt, and two weeks in Israel.

Their comprehensive and articulate report left little room for misunderstanding: "The Middle East Regional Cooperation (MERC) Program has achieved during its ten years of existence a remarkable record of success. Egyptian/Israeli scientific and technical cooperation has yielded significant achievements in the fields of agriculture, public health, and marine technology. The projects have dealt with subjects of high priority in which both Egyptian and Israeli efforts resulted in work of considerable utility to both countries. Good professional relationships have been established, as well as cordial personal friendships. Despite a background of political tensions and violence in the area, the scientific work was not affected significantly." This team attributed the program's success to the following factors:

1. The achievements of the U.S. academic entrepreneurs;
2. High-level host government support; and
3. Excellent Israeli and Egyptian coordinators.

The team had the following recommendations:
1. Formation of a U.S. Policy Oversight Board;
2. A Steering Committee for each project ("program" under our definition) in which we pioneered;
3. Clarification of the respective roles of the embassy and AID mission in Cairo;
4. Periodic formal meetings between the Egyptians and Israelis (as in our workshops)
5. Evenhandedness in U.S. administration of the program;
6. More attention at the top management level of AID; and
7. A management study to improve financial disbursement and accountability procedures.

To emphasize the last, the team stated, "The Program's productivity has been remarkable considering the loose manner in which projects are initiated, carried out, and evaluated."

The team did not, perhaps, pay as much attention to the overarching goal of tension reduction in the Middle East as might have been hoped for, considering their level of participation. This was not, however, part of their charge from AID, which itself is not under any particular mandate from Congress or the administration to seek that goal. The team observed that "AID has taken the position that its role as executor of a congressional initiative is not to formulate a strategy and then solicit submissions, but only to examine unsolicited proposals...." In other words, AID has not really been asked to reduce tensions in the Middle East, as such. The team did, however, recommend that "Opportunities for scientific collaboration involving additional Arab countries should be explored with suitable sensitivity and care as this becomes feasible."

Finally, the team noted what will be emphasized later in this paper concerning the ratio of the MERC Program's size compared to total U.S. aid to that region. "In fact, during the 10 years of MERC's regional program, total support for agricultural research added up to about $27 million; in contrast, the present bilateral program in Egypt includes $300 million over a five-year period for agricultural research alone."

The team perceptively realized something that this author has tried to emphasize: "Research on the part of U.S. institutions is not endorsed. Given the limited funds available to MERC, we feel that the maximum amount possible should be devoted directly to research by Egyptians and Israelis. We recommend that overhead costs be minimized and that separate research by U.S. institutions, ostensibly supplementing joint Egyptian/ Israeli endeavors, be precluded."

Their final recommendation was extremely penetrating. The team obviously recognized the need to expand to other disciplines and countries but not at the expense of losing the veterans who essentially hold the program together. They concluded, "As the political climate permits, however, priority should be given to new projects that would bring in other Arab countries."[6]

The most recent examination was conducted in July 1993 by the AGRIDEC Corporation. Their team included John H. Eriksen of Ithaca International, Limited; Stephan Grilli of the Department of Ocean Engineering of the University of Rhode Island; and Jean-Yves Mevel, an independent aquaculture consultant from Alabama. This review was limited to the MERC Marine Program. Their overall impression of the program is that "it was an excellent contribution to the successful melding of critical United States geo-political interests in the Middle East and quality scientific contributions to the solution of some of the area's development problems. The Program nurtured a favorable environment for increased contacts and cooperation between Egyptian and Israeli scientists. The essential factors which led to the overall success of the Program remain as portrayed in the last MERC program evaluation."[7] To these factors, the evaluation team would add one more: the maintenance by participants of a low-key, flexible approach to program development over the past 13 years.

This team penetrated somewhat more deeply into the workings of the program than their predecessors, finding the following:
1. There is little continuity in funding, retarding scientific progress.
2. Objectivity is lacking in the AID proposal review and selection process.
3. The role of the Americans should sharply diminish.
4. While the search for new faces should continue, the coordinating cadre should be maintained.
5. More junior scientists should be enrolled in the program.
6. American leadership is aging, and no obvious replacements are in sight.

This team broadened its perspective somewhat to consider the role of the program on a region-wide basis, concluding that the possibilities were significant. This may, in all likelihood, link to their other recommendation, strongly emphasized, that the role of the Middle East coordinators be strengthened vis-à-vis that of the Americans, who should be phased out.[8]

In summary, the degree of corroboration among all of the evaluations is surprising in some ways and unsurprising in others. They all appeared to feel that the program is achieving its objectives, that more of the policy initiative should be vested in the Egyptian and Israeli leaders, and that administration should be streamlined. The failure to dwell more on tension reduction overall can be attributed to a parallel subordination of these objectives in AID's own mandate from Congress.

AID's Evaluation Program Methodology

The U.S. Agency for International Development has evolved one of the most comprehensive techniques of project evaluation of any agency in Washington. This can be verified by accessing the basic *AID Evaluation Handbook* TM-3S:15.[9] The Evaluation Program's flagship is the Logical Framework (LOGFRAME) depicted in Figure 10. The LOGFRAME represents a sophisticated and very sincere effort to tie goals and objectives to results. It is viewed as an extremely effective vehicle from the perspective of a typical AID program, i.e., in agricultural or health terms, when the stock increase or curables can be accounted for arithmetically. Its effectiveness in some of the marine projects may vary depending on the tangibility of the project themselves. For instance, mariculture is amenable to the technique, because fish can be counted and sold. Fish sanitation is less adaptable to the technique.

When the Marine Program started, inasmuch as it was a trailblazer, the author was advised that he was pretty much on his own regarding an evaluation technique. Thus, the original LOGFRAMES may have been slightly primitive. Later on, about 1987, AID assigned a project evaluation specialist, Ms. Nina Vreeland, to the MERC Program to assist and guide the evaluations. She attended the definitive meeting at AID in 1989, but a number of follow-up applications for her guidance went unanswered. On the other hand, most of the AID officials assigned as project managers went out of their way to assist. Throughout the 15-year career of the Marine Program, we were never corrected in construction of these LOGFRAMES, so we assumed them to be adequate. A sample is included as Figure 10 on the following page.

For a program of this complexity, with its rather exotic aims, relying solely on formal evaluations may impart a degree of imbalance to the picture. Certainly the opinions of officials in the executive and legislative

Logical Framework: Seafood Safety

Narrative Summary	Objectively Verifiable Indicators	Means of Verification	Assumptions
Overall Goal: To bring about improvements in the health and safety of produced, marketed, and consumed seafood in Egypt and Israel	1. Health risk assessment of seafood safety. 2. Development of safety guide-lines and regulatory options. 3. Adoption of health and safety regulations.	1. Reduction in the levels of contaminants in the marketed seafood. 2. Improvements in the health statistics concerning seafood-related diseases.	1. Secure the cooperation of government regulatory agencies, fish production associations and consumer groups. 2. Ability of the regulatory agencies to adopt and enforce seafood safety controls.
Purpose: 1. Develop an overall assessment of the types, degree, and distribution of contaminants in the marketed fish. 2. Improve the effectiveness of fish decontamination procedures used by fish farmers. 3. Improve existing regulations and controls of seafood safety.	1. Establishment of a data bank for seafood safety. 2. Development of guidelines indicating advantages and limitations of current fish decontaminations procedures. 3. Development ofguidelines for improved fish decontamination procedures. 4. Development of guidelines for the regulation and control of seafood safety.	1. Project reports to AID Project Officer. 2. Communication of project findings to policy and decision makers, fish producers and the general public.	1. The same government officials, business repre-sentatives, and citizen groups will be able to participate throughout the project period. 2. Availability of good health statistics. 3. Accessibility to health data and other pertinent information.

Outputs:			
1. Information and referral systems on seafood safety. 2. Regulatory options for seafood safety. 3. Control scenarios for each regulatory option.	1. Database on seafood contamination and health data. 2. Maximum contaminant levels and health effect criteria for fish contaminants. 3. Acceptable risk and cost-benefit analyses for each regulatory option.	1. Interim and annual progress reports. 2. Project publications. 3. Workshop proceedings.	1. The collaborating institutions will fulfill their obligations in a timely fashion. 2. Project findings will be adequately disseminated by the relevant government agencies.
Inputs:			
1. Financial support for the US-AID. 2. Technical support from the collaborating institutions involved in the project. 3. Flexibility in modifying research methods and procedures, when necessary.	1. Qualified and well-trained project staff. 2. Adequate technical capabilities. 3. Quality assurance program to guarantee the validity and accuracy of research results.	1. Availability of technical and human resources, capable of project implementation. 2. Adequate management structure and procedures. 3. Adequate accounting and procurement capabilities.	1. Continuity of project support. 2. Ability to receive additional support in case of unforseen setbacks, accidents, etc. 3. No change in the attitude of the government agencies towards cooperation with our project.

Figure 10. Logical Framework: Seafood Safety

branches of government, whose assignments and interests are clearly to be served by successful implementation of the MERC Program, ought to be taken into account. Accordingly, a survey was prepared and issued to those persons in the House of Representatives and Senate most closely associated with the program. The questionnaire and responses are reproduced in Appendix D.

Finally, and possibly most important, the viewpoint of the sponsoring agency itself ought to weigh at least as heavily as those of the outsiders, whose appraisals were, after all, one-shot procedures. For this purpose, the administrator of AID was asked to provide his assessment of the program. I was informed that at that level, there was insufficiently close involvement with the program to be really helpful. On the other hand, the working-level representative, who handled MERC affairs on a day-to-day basis, could hardly be expected to enunciate policy for the agency.

Following considerable in-house discussion, I was informed that Gerald L. Kamens, who for nearly a decade bore the middle management responsibility for administration of the program, would speak for the agency. Emblematic of the superb manner in which he had conducted his previous assignment, Mr. Kamen's careful and comprehensive analysis is reproduced below.

AID's Goals

As previously stated, AID's goals shifted over the career of the program from domination by "togetherness" to "economic payoff" to "good science." These goals are enunciated in AID's most recent doctrine, promulgated in 1995 and capsulated in Appendix C.[10]

1. The "togetherness" theme resulted in tension reduction. It was quite easy to see how the interrelationships relaxed and became closer over the years, tending toward easy camaraderie.

2. "Economic payoffs," by definition, impose a longer range goal: The fish don't grow from 9:00 a.m. to 5:00 p.m., and immediate economic enhancement is simply not discernible, nor has it ever been in oceanographic programs. To bolster this argument one needs only to turn to the nine formal evaluations of America's National Sea Grant Program, which attempted to measure its cost-effectiveness as this country's first applied marine technology program.

3. "Good science" can, in theory, become a powerful tool in influencing tension reductions if it is clearly a reciprocal arrangement, i.e., one in which all participants teach, all participants learn, and all participants benefit. Candor requires the admission that this may indeed have taken place in one or another of the MERC programs, but it cannot be reported for the Marine Program per se.

Reorganization and "Mission Creep"

In attempting to penetrate the reason(s) for AID's shift in emphasis, one confronts a logical mix of personalities, reorganization, and the overall "Washington scene."

Most of the AID officials connected with the MERC Program over the years have been foreign service personnel. As such, they were usually well trained, competent, and peripatetic. A few personnel were civil service who sometimes exhibited a slightly different perspective of program management. I recorded the names of over thirty such persons with whom I dealt over the fifteen-year period.

During this period, I also witnessed at least three major reorganizations within the agency. There is no fundamental argument with reorganization, which can be dictated by the Washington scene, wherein, for instance, congressional demands for basic changes in program design and/or execution may cause realignment of existing forces. Empirically, however, it is noticeable that most reorganizations follow changes at the top, e.g., after elections and cabinet turnovers.

The literature on government organization and reorganization is mountainous. In the context of this book, therefore, let it suffice to resort to what is arguably the most pragmatic (if somewhat cynical) observation recorded on the subject by Dr. Harold Seidman, who was Assistant Director of the Office of Management and Budget during 1964 to 1968, later serving as consultant to the President's Advisory Committee on Executive Organization. His book, *Politics, Position, and Power,* opens with the following observation:

> Reorganization has become almost a religion in Washington. It has its
> symbol in the organization chart, old testament in the Hoover
> Commission Reports, high priesthood in the Bureau of the Budget,

and society for the propagation of the faith in sundry groups such as the Citizens Committee for the Hoover Report.

Reorganization is deemed synonymous with reform and reform with progress. Periodic reorganizations are prescribed if for no other purpose than to purify the bureaucratic blood and to prevent stagnation. Opposition to reorganization is evil and attributable, according to Mr. Hoover, to the "gang up, log-rolling tactics of the bureaus and their organized pressure groups."

For the true believer, reorganization can produce miracles; eliminate waste and save billions of dollars; restore to health and economic vigor a chronically ill maritime industry; abate noise at airports; control crime in the streets, to name but a few....[11]

The question that must be asked is, "Has reorganization helped or hindered the MERC Program?" While one hates to equivocate, the honest answer is that it can go either way. MERC is not a conventional program. It was thrust upon AID by Congress, and the agency has often pontificated optimum placement within its framework.

Personalities have ranged widely. The originally responsible official, Blaine Richardson, had little use for the assignment when it was first handed to him, but he reacted with outstanding alacrity, grace, efficiency, and judgment once the first proposal was in his hands. A dozen years later, his successor nine times removed, Henderson Patrick, was blessed with instant comprehension of new ideas, sophisticated judgment, and clear dedication to the program. This excellent official differed philosophically from some of his predecessors in that he adopted a course of action after careful thought, then worried about the minutiae and impedimenta later.

The matter of "Mission Creep" cannot be dealt with casually. In retrospect, ascendance of scientific excellence on AID's priority ladder was probably inevitable. Estimating the quantity and quality of in-house and sponsored research among federal government agencies is beyond the scope of this discussion, but it is clearly mountainous. With particular reference to the subject at hand, marine science was virtually unknown at the end of World War II, and the total federal budget for such research was on the order of $25 million.[12] It was, however, incorporated into the missions of 28 agencies by 1965, and the budget had climbed to $300

Figure 11. (Left to Right) Ravi Hochman, Mayor of Eilat, Prof. Hamed A.F. Gohar, Dr. Yuval Cohen, and Cong. James Scheuer at the celebration of Prof. Gohar's 82nd birthday. Warmth and camaraderie were evident everywhere during the gathering.

million![13] It is, after all, very hard for an agency chief or division director to eschew such glamorous activities as scientific research, particularly at appropriations hearings time.

While transfer of emphasis to scientific merit may have been questionable at the time of adoption of the doctrine, it is now unarguable. When the program began, AID officials were desperate for passable proposals and projects, while the budget for the MERC Program rose from $4 million to $7 million. During 1965, however, they faced over $100 million worth of proposals, not only allowing, but really forcing them to choose on the basis of scientific excellence, among other parameters. This is not a trivial problem, particularly in view of the loss of their travel funds budget, which prohibited on-site evaluation of what they were sponsoring.

In partial relief, I designed, and, with AID's blessing, executed a workshop of all of the MERC Project principal investigators in Washington, thus, in a sense, "bringing the mountain to Mohammed." According to AID officials, the procedure has proved extremely helpful in the management process.

At this time, therefore, with a sizable ratio of proposals to available dollars, AID cannot only afford, but is actually forced, to select and approve projects with great care and to give proper weight, not only to scientific excellence, but to economic and cultural payoff and potential for improving social relations and reducing tensions in the Middle East.

Setting the Pattern

Beyond argument, a major contribution of the Marine Program—perhaps its most important—was its trailblazing nature. As the first of the MERC Programs to get started, it set the pattern for process, including recruitment, planning, coordination, execution, and program control, which all of the other MERC Program component projects have followed, more or less closely. As the originator of the largest MERC Program, the CALAR Program, stated, "We watched how Bob Abel did it and decided to go in business for ourselves."[14]

The program, and the pattern that became its hallmark (as described in Chapter 3), have been brought to the attention of senators, representatives, and ranking officials in the State Department, Defense Department, and the National Security Council. American ambassadors in Jordan, Israel, Egypt, and Saudi Arabia have also examined the program's procedures and expressed satisfaction with its processes. Taking advantage of this, the author has been able to speak for the MERC concept in both houses of Congress. Since the program was legislatively inspired instead of being born in one or another executive agency, the result has been one of gratification to the legislators.

The Egyptians as Evaluation Indices

The Egyptian delegations to the program have proved a rather reliable barometer of tension reduction. The first meeting was held in the United States; otherwise, it would have been impossible. The next several meetings were divided between the United States and Cairo or Alexandria, as the Egyptians simply could not enter Israel. When held in Egypt, the meetings were usually confined to an obscure hotel, and the atmosphere might have been described as "furtive."

About the time of Dr. Eisawy's assumption of command of the Egyptian delegation, he decided to move some of the meetings to Israel. His confrontations with his Foreign Office are outside the scope of this study, but he did succeed. It gradually became customary for squads of up to a dozen Egyptian scientists to visit Haifa, Tel Aviv, Tiberias, and Eilat. Still later, smaller groups visited the Israeli laboratory to study and participate in the Israelis' experimental procedures. Dr. Serruya's technique of continuing to send her scientists to Egypt is described later.

Other Countries

One of the guiding precepts of the program has been to extend it to countries other than Egypt. Since AID interpreted the original congressional dictum as referring only to Israel and Egypt, private monies had to be raised to work with the Jordanians and Saudis. This, of course, was all to the good. The nature and power of this program's concept render it capable of attracting almost all of the countries in the Islamic world!

Obviously, substantiation of the argument is called for. The attitude of the Jordanians and their willingness not only to participate but to accelerate the pace of the program is but a single example. The nature of conversations with the Saudis has confirmed the efficacy of pursuing this track. The ease of dealing with the Tunisians and Moroccans has been amply demonstrated not only in the appended letter from Hatem Atallah, but by several of the other MERC project directors in their own dealings.

The problem plainly is *time!* This raises the issue of the perfect MERC project director. He or she must have the time to travel and conduct the necessary negotiations with cognizant officials in these countries. A visit every four to six months for a couple of days simply does not do the job (nor does it enable one to learn Arabic—a highly useful adjunct to the job). Unfortunately, the other necessary characteristic is prestige. Arab officials, like their counterparts in other countries, do not wish to deal with menials.

By logical deduction, it becomes evident that the ideal administrator of a MERC project must be a reasonably high-level official who has plenty of time to do the work.

This person does not exist, and this is perhaps the greatest built-in drawback to the MERC concept. It has been frustrating, to say the least, to know that people are interested and ready to collaborate in these kinds of projects and yet not have the time to do anything about it. Also, candor requires the admission that the problem is not a matter of money. Imagination and a little spadework marry conveniently to unearth funds for travel when such funds are needed, and, more to the point, can be shown to be usefully applied in a good cause.

Other Funding

This leads naturally to assessment of "other" funding as a useful index of measurement of the program's (perceived) success. To date, the program has received ancillary funding from the U.S. Environmental Protection Agency, the Rockefeller Foundation (a major contributor), and the Hanson, Scheuer, and Dorot foundations, as well as from "friends" of the program. Cursory investigations seem to indicate that many other sources of funding would become available, given time on the part of the program's administrators.

It is also very important, at this point, to invite attention to the considerable contributions matched by the Israeli and Egyptian governments, in kind, through salary, facility, and equipment donations.

Government vs. Nongovernment Functionaries

A question that has screamed for attention from the beginning relates to the best-equipped instrumentality for this type of program. At this time, most of the MERC Program projects are government-to-government, involving, for example, the U.S. Department of Agriculture and the National Institutes of Health on the U.S. side. The first two projects to get off the ground, however, were nongovernmental (NGO) in nature: the Marine and Cooperative Arid Lands Research projects.

Government-conducted programs have certain built-in advantages. For one thing, they may have relatively unlimited travel funds (depending on their position at the time). For another, they can draw on more human resources for whatever job is involved. A third advantage lies in the government-wide communications network, which not only offers them easier access to the embassies (including free telephone calls) but recognition upon entering said embassies.

The advantage of the NGO operation, although less tangible, is nonetheless formidable.

The MERC Program, by its very nature, involves some risks at the diplomatic level. Consequently, it's very convenient and easy for embassy officials to wash their hands over a mistake made by a private individual, whose connections to the diplomatic community are, at best, nebulous. By the same reasoning, they are able to capitalize on whatever communications gains have been attained by the same private individual- and they are very welcome to it.

Failures

Since the closure of the Garden of Eden, the error-free program has never existed. The MERC Marine Program is no exception. The most glaring failures during its career, however, have had some interesting spin-offs.

The first major failure occurred during the Seafood Safety Project, wherein the Israelis were to be responsible for the heavy metal analyses and the Egyptians for the organic contaminants analyses. The two groups never really got together, as pointed out by Robinson and Mevli. Yet Dr. Charia Naguib, the Egyptian principal investigator, proved to be the most magnificent hostess in Egypt upon arrival of the Israeli team; finally, two years later, she did in fact venture into the "forbidden territory."

The second and most serious failure occurred as part of the Climate Prediction Program, when the exigencies of the U.S. procurement regulatory system lost 19 of the 36 months allotted to this project. A coalition of scientists from the United States, Turkey, Israel, and Egypt is currently exploring the possibilities of exhuming the project for further development.

Enforcement vs. Encouragement

As previously described, Dr. Patrick Clawson has offered the most cogent and comprehensive recommendations for enforced cooperation vis-à-vis suggested or encouraged cooperation. His concept of a collaborative airport at Eilat/Aqaba, for instance, in which three countries would have to share common facilities such as runways, but perhaps entering and exiting through three different access points, must be taken seriously. The MERC Program, to the best of our knowledge, however, has operated on the suggestive rather than the mandated principle. Perhaps there is a place for both types of project initiation.

Level of Support

This author has never examined a report of a federal program that did not recommend an increased level of funding. Responsible analysis, however, must always ask the question: "Where is the money to come from?"

As nearly as can be determined at this time, the MERC Program overall draws about 1/10 of 1 percent of the total funding conveyed from the United States to the Middle East each year. This amounts to the current appropriations level of $7 million. Should the program be adjudged worthy of an infusion of funds to, say, 2/10 of 1 percent of our Middle East funding, this would double the MERC appropriation to $14 million. In fact, to reach the proper perspective, every additional million dollars transferred from our normal Middle East expenditures each year would cut that budget by about 0.05 percent. The whole point of this exercise is to avoid the usual procedure of requesting new money, because there isn't any more.

Conclusion: Measuring Tension Reduction

For the purposes of this study, the measurement "campaign" has been categorized according to "external" reviews (outside, formal reviews) and "internal" reviews. Part of the internal evaluation process has been by inference, as described by the anecdotes in the previous chapter; the rest of the process is based on interviews and solicited and unsolicited views from persons who have had occasion to deal with the program from one or another vantage point. These are organized into a reasonably coherent progression in the following chapter.

All of the four formal reviews have stated that the Marine Program seems to have carried out its mission of bringing people together from Egypt and Israel in a series of common causes.

High-level informal opinions appear to bear out the formal reviews. Egyptian Prime Minister Yousef Walli and Israeli Prime Minister Shimon Peres are on the record as thinking highly of both the concept of regional cooperation and the manner in which the projects were carrying it out. These thoughts have been conveyed in clear terms directly to the author.[15]

Can the program be said to have had an influence on the Jordan-Israel peace process? No. The project leaders lost that glorious opportunity during 1988–93 in maneuvering a proposal when they should have been doing the work.

Viewed in broad perspective, the MERC Program, particularly the Marine Program, has accomplished many things. It would be fatuous to try to equate a program of this size to the massive aid given to the region by the United States, to say nothing of Japan and the rest of the industrial nations. All of the clues developed in the preceding pages, however, point to returns far beyond the original investment, and to an excellent future for the program, if sensible management is sustained.

Epilogue: Signposts Along the Pathway to Peace

Over the course of the Marine Program, a number of brief, isolated events occurred which, though perhaps meaningless in themselves, if taken together may indicate the growing camaraderie so vital to establishing good relationships, whether they be between croquet teams or countries.

The very first meeting held under the program's auspices (perhaps the first ever between Israeli and Arab scientific teams) took place in San Diego, California, in August 1980, under the sponsorship of the Hanson Foundation. As might well be imagined, the first session started in a cool manner, with the Egyptians suggesting that the affair be conducted as if it were a plenary session of a United Nations working group. The hosts were at a loss as to how to get the groups together, when Admiral Yohay Ben Nun, director general of the Israeli Institute of Oceanographic and Limnological Research, and leader of the Israeli contingent, noticed an Egyptian scientist at the coffee urn, brought with him an Israeli colleague, and engaged the Egyptian in conversation. When he was satisfied that the two other scientists' conversation had become self-sustaining, the admiral went off to find more candidates to continue the campaign. Thus it was that "coffee urn" diplomacy broke the ice. By the end of the four-day meeting, practically all tensions had been broken between the two parties and joint planning for their respective projects was well underway.

Admiral Ben Nun resigned as director general soon after, yielding his post to Dr. Collette Serruya. During her tenure, while relations between the two countries were still strained, she maintained a practice of sending her scientists to visit their respective opposite numbers in Cairo and Alexandria, to keep communications open. In the process, the scientists on the Shore Processes Project, Drs. Abraham Golik (Israel) and Ahmed Khafagi (Egypt), developed a very special relationship, during which Dr. Golik visited Alexandria eight times to conduct their joint project. In about the fifth year of the project, when a workshop including all of the scientists in the program was scheduled in Egypt, the Egyptian ambassador to Israel was temporarily recalled. When the charge d'affaires, as acting ambassador, confronted the Israelis' visa applications, he was struck by Golik's record of visitations. Suspecting involvement of an other-than-legitimate nature, he delayed all of the visa applications until the matter could be cleared up, which was precisely one day before the meeting was to start.

In turn, Dr. Khafagi was the first of the Egyptian group to visit Israel. The hospitality accorded him included a meeting with Israel's minister of energy and infrastructure, who, learning of Khafagi's background as an experienced coastal engineer, invited him to inspect the beaches of Tel Aviv, where officials were dealing with a vexing silting problem. During the course of the interchanges, Dr. Khafagi was offered, and accepted, a consultantship from the Israeli government (to our knowledge, the first in Israel's history) to solve the beach deterioration problems.

The above heartening incidents notwithstanding, it still appeared impossible, even after five years of the program, for the Egyptians to visit Israel in groups. In 1985, Dr. A.R. Bayoumi, the Egyptian coordinator of the program, died most tragically. His position was assumed by Dr. Ahmed Mohammed Eisawy. Dr. Eisawy immediately demonstrated both the talent and the will to "fight the system." Within weeks following his assumption of the coordinator's role, he led a team of 10 Egyptian scientists to the program's next workshop, in Haifa. The team toured all of the Israelis' oceanographic facilities and forged yet another set of friendships and alliances.

The following year, in 1986, the author visited Jordan for the first time. He was advised by U.S. Ambassador Roscoe Suddarth that such a visit was sensitive, occurring as it did during very tense times. It was clear that American amateurs were not particularly welcome in the entire

Figure 12. Israeli and Egyptian scientists, holding meetings along the Nile, pause for a photograph. The Israelis wearing blue/white and the Egyptians wearing red/black/white identical T-shirts inscribed in English and hieroglyphics, "Love Dr. Bob!"

region. Just a year later, however, the same ambassador suggested to the author not only that he was apparently on the right track but that his future visits and relationships would be strongly supported by the U.S. Embassy. It was just after that episode that Jordan became represented on our Steering Committee, de facto, for the ensuing years of the program, and played a key role in planning the Aqaba Program.

In 1988, Dr. Khafagi asked the author to act as go-between for a program under consideration by the Egyptian Irrigation Ministry. The ministry wanted to explore the possibilities of a joint geological survey with Israel for deep water tables under the Negev and Sinai. In answer to his request, the author was advised by the Israeli minister that he had a total "green light" to open negotiations with the Egyptians, and the Israeli government would support the project enthusiastically. (Unfortunately, such things take time, and the project is still in the "thinking" stage.)

In 1989, during another workshop in Haifa, the Israeli coordinator informed the group that Deputy Prime Minister Shimon Peres happened to be visiting; would the group like to meet him? Over the author's doubts, the Egyptian coordinator, Dr. Eisawy, responded enthusiastically and engaged the deputy prime minister in conversation for 40 minutes after which time Mr. Peres stated, "This is magnificent!" Without stopping for breath, Dr. Eisawy had offered a vision of an Israeli-Egyptian brotherhood developing, followed by recruitment of, first, the other Middle Eastern countries, and then the African nations, drawn by the natural bonds of technical cooperation. This was truly a spectacular performance.

In 1990, in conjunction with a congressional delegation's visit, the entire group of Israeli and Egyptian scientists met at Eilat, as guests of the IOLR's National Center for Mariculture. The first order of business was to recognize the eighty-second birthday of the Egyptian delegation's leader, Dr. Hamid Gohar (since deceased), with a meter-diameter cake. Then Dr. Yuval Cohen, the Israeli coordinator, announced that the Israelis were having a problem devising a plan to equal the hospitality that they had received in Egypt during the previous workshop. Accordingly, they had planned a floor show, which would be performed in Arabic, in honor of their Egyptian brothers. At that point, three of Egypt's leading oceanographers came into the room, chanting about an old, fat, bald American who had recruited a bunch of poor scientists into a crazy program. But the crazy program appeared to be working and they were all having a fine time working together. They were all dressed in identical T-shirts, inscribed in hieroglyphics and English, "Love Dr. Bob." This was possibly the most purely emotional experience of the author's career.

Throughout the all-too-brief history of the MERC Marine Program, the workshops have been wonderfully characterized by confrontation, but between disciplines and projects, never between national delegations. This offers quiet evidence of the value of the MERC process.

Notes

1.   Public Law 95-384 of September 26, 1978, "International Security Assistance Act of 1978," U.S. Congress, Washington, D.C., 1978.
2.   Personal conversation with Joseph Wheeler, Acting Administrator, Agency for International Development, April 1980.
3.   Richmond, Addison, "Normalization and its Implications-The Development of Relations Between Egypt and Israel Since 1977." Executive Seminar in National and International Affairs, U.S. Department of State, Washington, D.C., 1981.
4.   Pollack, Herman, and Clarence Idyll, "Evaluation-Cooperative Marine Technology Program for the Middle East." Prepared for AID, George Washington University, Washington, D.C., 1983.

5. Busch, Charles and Conrad Recksiek, "Mid-Term Evaluation of the Cooperative Marine Technology Program for the Middle East (290-0190)," by the RONCO Corporation, Washington, D.C., 1985.
6. Kontos, William, William Reinke, and Quentin West, "Review of Middle East Regional Cooperation Program (Project No. 398-0158.25)," by Devres, Inc., Washington, D.C., 1991.
7. Ibid.
8. Eriksen, John, Stephan Grilli, and Jean-Yves Mevel, "The Cooperative Marine Technology Program for the Middle East. Phase III-A. Final Evaluation Report," by AGRIDEC, Inc., Miami, 1993.
9. AID Evaluation Handbook TM–35:15, "A.I.D. Program Design and Evaluation Methodology Report No. 7," April 1989, Agency for International Development, Washington, D.C., 1989.
10. U.S. Agency for International Development, "The Middle East Regional Cooperative Program—Introduction and Guidelines for Proposals," USAID, Washington, D.C., 1994.
11. Seidman, Harold, *Politics, Position, & Power*, Oxford University Press, New York, 1970.
12. National Oceanographic Program Fiscal Year, 1962, Interagency Committee on Oceanography Pamphlet #2, A report from the President to the Congress, March 1961, Executive Office of the President, 1961.
13. National Oceanographic Program Fiscal Year, 1966, Interagency Committee on Oceanography Pamphlet #17, A report from the President to the Congress, January 1965, Executive Office of the President, 1965
14. Personal conversation with Joseph Wheeler, April 1980.
15. Richmond, Addison, op. cit.

5. Conclusions and Recommendations

As gleaned from the literature (Chapter 1), personal contacts, the thoughts and observations of my colleagues in the program, and personal experience, and as screened through the program's analysis (Chapter 4) , several suggestions come to mind regarding how the Middle East Regional Cooperation Program can be further utilized in the interests of peace in the Middle East. (Of course, these suggestions may well be overtaken by events in the interval between pen and print.)

1. All of the formal AID evaluations concurred that the MERC Marine Program appears to be working well and achieving its objectives. The latest analysis identified administrative flaws that have mainly been adjusted. The overall assessment of the MERC Program conducted so perceptively by the Devres Corporation[1] concluded that not only the Marine Program but to a greater or lesser degree all of the MERC programs appeared to be making fair, satisfactory, or excellent progress.

2. A natural outgrowth of the above (and indeed of any analytical process) is the question, Does the program deserve increased funding? The author has never reviewed a report of a government program that did not recommend greater funding. These days, however, it's considerably more realistic to accompany such recommendations with suggestions as to funding sources. Fischer, Rodrik, and Tuma[2] have recognized the disparity in military spending between the Middle Eastern nations (15 percent) and the industrial nations (5 percent). If it is so logical for these countries to begin drastic reductions in their military spending, why should it make any less sense for the United States to do likewise regarding its foreign aid to these same countries?

    For instance, if the United States currently gives the Middle Eastern countries an aggregate of \$3 billion, a large percentage of which is spent on the military, would it be so drastic to double the 0.1 percent of foreign aid that is currently spent on regional cooperation to 0.2 percent? This, then, is offered as a rather modest fiscal recommendation.

3. As all the evaluation contractors have observed, and as has become very apparent, the teams in the Middle Eastern countries have learned to work exceptionally well together. They have absorbed the American techniques of policy making and execution, and they understand very well the administrative routing sequence of planning, coordination, execution, and control. At least in the Marine Program, the participants have become sophisticated in their project accomplishment. It is therefore concluded that increasing responsibility for program design and conduct should transfer from the American universities and government agencies to their Middle East counterparts. While from AID's perspective it is still important to maintain an American instrumentality as fiscal functionary, there is no reason why the other authorities and responsibilities cannot proceed eastward. This recommendation is highlighted in the Devres report previously described.

4. By the same reasoning, a vastly increased share of program funds must go to the Middle East, for which they were intended. Congress has made clear its intent that this program was not to be another funding source for American institutions. The MERC Marine Program can easily qualify as a case in point. An inordinate share of the total funding had to be assigned to "management" (meaning American management) owing to the nature of the process. As institutions' indirect cost rates climbed, this appeared increasingly nugatory, and at the first opportunity the program was ceded to Texas A&M University, whose superior grants handling ability presumably qualified it to handle such programs. (In retrospect, comparative analysis indicates a much smaller gain than had been supposed earlier.)

    Whatever the factors, AID now confronts more and better proposals with the same funds as half a decade ago. It must, therefore, assign management cost control very high priority in ranking proposals.

5. It is true that during the first decade of its tenure the MERC Program seemed to be monopolized by a very few contractors who appeared to have mastered the intricacies of dealing with Israelis and Arabs. The program, however, was never intended for "funding in perpetuity." On the other hand, there can be no doubt of the value of maintaining at least part of the cadres who

proved the most successful in developing cooperation and recruiting others to this banner. Accordingly, the government must continue to seek an optimum balance between the need to expand the program by identifying and recruiting new people and groups and the need to retain some of the "old hands." The most reasonable, viable suggestion advanced so far is that the Americans who have benefited measurably from the program should donate their experience and expertise to newly arriving organizations that can supply new blood. This is the role adopted by the author.

6. If the program's effect on tension reduction is to become more widely recognized, it must be brought to the attention of top management in the participating countries. This is normally best accomplished at the same level in this country. Paradoxically, however, knowledge of the program appears to be limited to ever-lower management levels at AID over recent years.

Future aims include the following:

1. Adding new technologies, institutions, and people to the program, to spread its beneficial influence throughout as many communities as possible in the two countries;

2. Encouraging as many scientists as possible to visit each other's country;

3. Conveying the program's benefits to other Middle Eastern and African countries, in an effort to persuade them to join the program; and

4. Translating the scientific achievements into economic and cultural gains.

As we look to the future, the program's leaders don't envision a smoothly rising curve of acceptance and participation. We would predict, rather, a sort of step-like movement, as one after another the social and financial barriers give way to good fellowship, beneficial technology, and—above all—common sense.

In summary, we, the program's practitioners, believe we are in the process of demonstrating what history may term the ocean's greatest gift to humanity: Peace!

A necessary and proper homage must be paid to all those who designed and executed the MERC Program in Washington, D.C.—from its author, Representative Henry Waxman, through the congressional committees that developed and passed the amendment to the Foreign

Assistance Act to the agency to which it was assigned, the U.S. Agency for International Development. As founder of the initial MERC Program, this author acknowledges that those first steps would have been impossible without their help.

Finally, amidst all the sweat and strain, and the toil and turmoil attendant upon conducting a program of this nature, it has all somehow seemed worthwhile—very worthwhile.

Appendix A

Correspondence from the Higher
Council on Science and Technology
of the Kingdom of Jordan

بسم الله الرحمن الرحيم

المجلس الأعلى للعلوم والتكنولوجيا

The Higher Council for Science and Technology

General Secretariat   الأمانة العامة

Ref : 1 /2/1/1581
Date: 31/Oct/1993.

Dr. R. B. Abel
Director, International Programs
Stevens Institute of Technology
711 Hudson Str. Hoboken
N.J. 07030 USA

FAX NO: (701) 216-8214

Dear Dr. Abel,

Thank for your letter of Sept 7, 1993. Dr Wahbeh has our full confidence as country's coordinator for Jordan in the proposed marine program. He will continue to represent HCST and will work closely with Yarmouk University and the University of Jordan (at the Aqaba Marine Station) to implement the project.

I hope that HCST will be kept up to date with the progress of the project and that interim reports and technical information will be periodically provided to us. I also understand from Dr. Wahbeh that no financial or administrative commitments are required from us.
Wishing you success in your endeavors, please accept my best wishes.

Sincerely Yours,

Hani Mulki
Secretary General

Tel. 840401 - Tlx 23019 TECHOC JO · Cable : TAKANA Amman - Fax :840589 - P.O.Box 16 jubaiha - Jordan

The Higher Council for Science and Technology

Ref.: 1/50/642

Date: July 1990

RECEIVED AUG 1 0 1990

Dr. Robert B. Abel
President - New Jersey Marine Sciences Consortium
Sandy Hook Executive Office
Building 22, Fort Hancock, NJ 07732
U.S.

Dear Dr. Abel,

In my follow-up on studies on the Gulf of Aqaba and the potential for joint research of a standard capable of attracting the highest level of international financial backing, I should like to affirm that the Higher Council nominates the Marine Science Station in Aqaba as our representative in any integrated program in this sphere. I believe that you have already been supplied with various relevant research projects undertaken and proposed by the Marine Science Station, specifically following the specialized Seminar they held in Aqaba in May 1989, which was attended by researchers from Egypt and the U.S. alongside local marine biologists/ecologists/researchers.

To this end, I am enclosing a copy of the Marine Science Station joint project paper on **Oceanographic Studies of the Gulf of Aqaba** as forwarded to me by Dr. Muhammad A. Wahbeh, Director of the Aqaba Marine Science Station and Associate Professor, Marine Ecology. The Station has been instrumental in the formulation of the joint project drive and is the Jordanian body specialized in marine sciences, joining the efforts of two of Jordan's universities as well as a wide spectrum of specialists over the years.

I am sure that you will find Dr. Wahbeh an able partner in your efforts for the marine welfare of this region.

Yours sincerely,

Dr. Abdullah Toukan
HCST Secretary General

cc. Dr. Muhammad Wahbeh, Director, Marine Science Station, P.O.B. 195, Aqaba

Appendix B

Protocol for the Conduct of the Cooperative Marine Technology Program for the Middle East

**PROTOCOL FOR THE CONDUCT OF
THE COOPERATIVE MARINE TECHNOLOGY PROGRAM FOR THE MIDDLE EAST**

A.   PREAMBLE

Toward the objective of accommodating the conduct of a cooperative technology program to its maturity and growth, its leaders have agreed upon certain terms. These terms, or frames of reference, will be useful in clarifying communications and the work flow process among the program's participants. In this manner, it provides agreed-upon guidelines for future conduct of the program.

It is intended for the use of participants in this program only and for information to others who are interested. It may not substitute, or contravene the regular provisions of the AID Program in any way.

Although they recognize the need to subscribe to the wishes of the program sponsor, e.g., the U.S. Agency for International Development, the country coordinators must accept a large degree of responsibility in cooperation with the program's general manager and chief scientist in the USA for design, coordination, direction, and control of the program. Toward this purpose, therefore, the program Steering Committee was established. A final purpose of this document is to clarify and memorialize the authorities, responsibilities, and usual functions of everyone involved in the program. <u>Nothing in this protocol, however, is intended in any way whatsoever to prevent or impede the creation or execution of other programs</u>.

B.   POLICY

1.   Policy communications will flow through the country coordinators.

2.   Communications concerning scientific and technical matters will, of course, proceed among any and all participants in a normal defined manner.

3.   Requests for program arrangements, such as Steering Committee meetings, are considered matters of policy.

4.   New projects within the program are considered matters of policy.

C.   DOCUMENTS

1.   All formal documents should be reviewed by the country coordinators and chief scientists prior to forwarding to sponsors. This includes, inter alia:

   a. Steering Committee minutes;

   b. Proposals;

In this regard, it is clearly in the country coordinators' best interests to foster good communications among the participating scientists during the proposal preparation and later processes.

2.   Project proposals should be reviewed and screened by the Steering Committee, conveyed thereto by the country coordinators;

3.   In turn, the coordinators are responsible for reviewing and editing, in a reasonable period of time, all documents sent to them by the chief scientists and general manager;

4.   Responsibility for editing the annual/semi annual reports is the chief scientist's and general manager's;

5.   Proposals should receive peer review prior to inclusion in the final proposal document. The process will be facilitated by the Steering Committee.

D.   **MEETINGS**

1.   All participating scientists are encouraged to meet - especially inter-country, as often as possible.
2.   Steering Committee meetings may be recommended by any of the Steering Committee members, respecting program policy and/or management.

   a.   Meetings will be convened, however, by the general manager, unless delegated by him otherwise. This relates particularly to Steering Committee meetings.

   b.   Workshops or multi-participant meetings are convened by the chief scientists.

3.   According to U.S. AID regulations for all sponsored programs, prospective travel must be requested via the Principal Investigator at least 3 weeks in advance of the travel. Shorter notice must be justified. Required data include: a. name of traveler(s); b. destination; c. dates of travel; and d. purpose of travel.

E.   **FUNDING AND ACCOUNTING**

1.   Since the AID contracting U.S. institution will normally house the chief scientist, all financial reports should be submitted to his institution. That institution, in turn, is responsible for keeping the general manager informed concerning fund usage rates and requests.

2.   The general manager is charged with responsibility for locating new funding sources and/or increasing existing sources. Chief scientists and country coordinators should assist as much as possible.

3.   Budgets should originate with the project Proposer. They should be reviewed by the Steering Committee to ensure conformance with recognized or reasonable limitations.

4.   During the process of budget formulation, the country coordinators should suggest to the Steering Committee what accommodations - in their view - might be helpful in finally arriving at a program budget that stays within the estimated limit overall and is reasonably balanced among countries, projects, and object classes. This in no way assigns a veto power to the country coordinators.

After the budget has been constructed to the satisfaction of the Steering Committee, it may be altered only in the event of reductions by the USAID. In such cases, the general manager will have the Steering Committee's delegated authority to apply the reductions pro rata, i.e., across the board.

F.   **PEER REVIEWS**

1.   Peer reviews shall be conducted for each of the projects submitted to prospective sponsors. This desirable process has the effect of:

   a.   Screening out projects which are scientifically inferior;

   b.   Strengthening the Steering Committee's position vis-a-vis the sponsoring agency.

2.   The peer review process shall be conducted along conventional lines (i.e., adhering primarily to the technique of the Sea Grant Program.)

   a.   The process will be conducted by the general manager, who, in consultation with the chief scientists, will send the candidate proposals to appropriate reviewers;

   b.   After determining a satisfactory consensus of the reviews, the general manager will return the reviewed projects to the Steering Committee for final assembly of the proposal package.

G.   **RESPECTIVE ROLES OF THE PROGRAM'S PARTICIPANTS**

1.   <u>The project scientists and their leaders, the principal investigators</u>, are the backbone of the program. They will conduct their scientific projects according to universally accepted terms of scientific comportment. In the special case of this program, however, they have the added responsibility of collaborating with their partners in the opposite country to ensure their work is:

   a. coordinated;

   b. complementary, rather than duplicated;

   c. cohesive, i.e., minimizing gaps in the process.

   Every effort will be made to maximize:

   a. visits to the partner laboratory;

   b. couplings of future activity;

   c. joint publication;

   d. assistance with graduate students;

3

e. coordinated responsiveness to special AID requirements.

In this particular regard, they should work with their respective country coordinators in responding to requests for reports on: sustainability; and economic benefits assessments.

2.   <u>The country coordinators</u>, in the final analysis, hold the program's real authority. They are responsible for:

a.   maintaining optimum interrelations with the cooperating country counterparts;

b.   achieving an excellent program package, reflecting:

    i.   coordinated components

    ii.   mutually satisfactory budgets

    iii.   response to the sponsor's needs

    iv.   broadening of the partnership by introducing new scientists and institutions to the program.

c.   ensuring timely and accurate reporting, referring to

    i.   financial documents

    ii.   semiannual and annual reports

d.   assisting the chief scientist and general manager in selecting dates and places for Steering Committee meetings and workshops.

e.   compiling and nominating project proposals to the Steering Committee (as detailed in paragraphs C 1, 2 and 3, above).

f.   collaborating fully in the proposal preparation process.

4.   <u>The program's general manager</u> will have the following authorities and responsibilities:

a.   initiating calls for, and chairing, Steering Committee meetings;

b.   acting as rapporteur at such meetings, unless he/she delegates this function;

c.   maintaining primary contact with the sponsoring agency/agencies;

d.   ensuring continuance of the program's objectives.

e.   ensuring that responsible American authorities in the host countries remain aware of the program's progress;

f.   exercising general coordination among the chief scientists and country coordinators;

g.   continuing to seek sources of augmenting support.

____
H.K. Badawi, Egypt

____
Y. Cohen, Israel

____
S.Z. El-Sayed, USA

____
R.B. Abel, USA

____
A.I. El Ibiary, Egypt

ENCL3PRO.DMD
1/12/94

Appendix C

**Abstract of the AID Middle East Regional
Cooperation Program**

THE MIDDLE EAST REGIONAL COOPERATION PROGRAM
(MERC)[1]

<u>**MERC**</u>

CONTENTS: I.   Introduction
II. Guidelines for Invited Proposals
III. Guidelines for Preliminary Proposals

---

[1]   This document provides information and guidelines for individuals or groups interested in preparing unsolicited grant proposals to the MERC Program for funding consideration. Issued in December 1994, this document supersedes prior versions and reflects the evolution of the MERC Program as it adapts to both reflect and support the evolving prospects and opportunities for the promotion of Middle East regional cooperation. Interest in and competition for MERC funding in recent periods has grown significantly, a trend expected to continue. For those familiar or acquainted with the MERC Program from earlier periods, there is much that remains familiar in this document, but there also is much that is new, enhanced, or more specifically defined. This document is intended to provide all interested parties with a clear understanding of MERC Program goals, what is important to a good proposal, and how to justify it in convincing terms.

-2-

I.   INTRODUCTION

***The MERC Program supports collaboration among Israel and its Arab
neighbors on common priority economic and social development
problems.***

Among key MERC Program review criteria are: contribution to the
Middle East Peace Process; degree of true collaboration;
development impact; technical quality of proposed activities;
potential for sustainability. (Cf. Guidelines, below.)

MERC projects may be funded for up to five years with maximum
MERC funding per project at $3 million. (Increasingly, approved
MERC grants are smaller than maximum funding limits).

    A.   MERC Program Premises. The basic **premise** of the MERC
program is that people who work together in a true collaborative
manner to solve common problems or to develop shared
opportunities substantially enhance knowledge and understanding
of each other, of their respective cultures and heritages, and of
their common goals and aspirations.

A **further premise** of the MERC program is that participating
country sectoral development programs are strengthened and
enhanced by regional cooperation projects which bring together
national experts and expertise in collaborative technological,
scientific, or other important efforts focused on common economic
or social development priorities.[2] A **corollary** is that if
successful, regional cooperation projects can help to attract
additional financial resources, public or private, national or
international, to common economic or social development programs.

Projects supported by the MERC program, the results produced by
those projects, and those participating in them are very likely

----

    [2] As Middle East relations evolve, opportunities are opening for
countries to progress faster and more equitably by working together rather than
by working in parallel but in isolation from each other. Examples might include
cooperation in weather prediction, managing coastal and water resources, in
identification of geological resources and seismological risks, control of
diseases/pests which respect no borders, expanding telecommunication networks
(networking more than one nation), and development of economic cooperation and
trade based on comparative advantage, among others. Regional cooperative
programs can support sustainable development through technology transfer or joint
research on common problems and resources, to data sharing, to agreement on
common technological standards. The MERC Program is open to all such proposals.
Neither these examples nor the traditional fields of MERC projects are exhaustive
of possibilities.

-3-

to become *important examples* and focal points for the development and spread of further mutual understanding to colleagues within participating institutions and nations, and even to other entities within the region.

    B. Regional Cooperation. *Active, focused, and broadly based regional cooperation* among the countries of the Middle East is the **fundamental goal** of the MERC program. Thus defined, regional cooperation is the principal, *essential criterion* for MERC project proposals.

Regional cooperation is an integral feature or characteristic of all stages of MERC project activities, from conceptualization to planning to implementation to completion.

MERC projects *join experts of the region in cooperative efforts* to solve priority economic and social development problems or develop or advance shared economic and social development opportunities. In each MERC project experts from one or more Israeli institutions and experts from institutions in one or more countries of the Middle East region combine and unite their expertise and efforts.

Regional cooperation can take many forms, e.g., collaborative data gathering and analysis of systems that cross the national boundaries of the participating countries; homogenization of scientific and technological systems to facilitate interchanges among the collaborating countries; collaborative work in which experts with complementary skills from the different countries work cooperatively and collegially to resolve a common problem; and many others as well.

A *U.S. institution may join* these regional cooperation projects as facilitator, participant[3], or mentor; or, one or more individual U.S. experts, without involvement of a U.S. institution, may play key collaborative roles in regional cooperation projects. Project proposals from consortia without a U.S. institution should demonstrate strong and proven management and should not require supplemental management from USAID in lieu of a U.S. partner.

    C.   MERC Project Themes/Sectors.   *Cooperative technology*

---

[3]   It is a general principle of the MERC program that the main technical, scientific or other expert work to be undertaken should be implemented by the Middle East country participants unless a convincing case is made that the direct involvement of the U.S. participant in such work is essential.

-4-

development, adaptation and exchange, and research collaboration
have been principal themes of MERC projects. Technical
assistance within a MERC project from one country to another may
be a part of such projects but the MERC program does not support
technical assistance projects ***per se***.

MERC projects ***are not restricted to specific sectors***. MERC
project activities contribute directly to achieving priority
national economic and social development objectives or to
developing solutions to priority development problems in each
participating Middle East country.

MERC project activities to the extent possible ***are consistent
with USAID's strategic program objectives (viz., Protecting the
Environment; Building Democracy; Stabilizing World Population
Growth and Protecting Human Health; and Encouraging Broad-based
Economic Growth)*** and with USAID management concerns in those
countries with USAID bilateral programs.

MERC project activities offer great likelihood of ***sustainability***
because of their relevance and value to participants and
beneficiaries. MERC increasingly evaluates proposals on the
likelihood that new collaborations established by MERC funding
can continue productively even after MERC funding ends.

MERC project activities--and their results--ideally ***have a high
degree of visibility***, in addition to their technical, scientific
or other merit, in order to promote further interest in and
support of Middle East regional cooperation.

     D.   <u>Development Impact.</u> MERC projects make a ***substantial
development contribution*** to the sector of focus in participating
countries. This significant furthering of priority development
objectives is the dominant justification for MERC projects.
***Regional cooperation (cf. above) is fundamental but not
sufficient***. MERC projects are sound, quality development
undertakings reflecting and matching development priorities and
satisfying development investment criteria, factors which are
more important than high-level endorsements.[4]

Proposals to the MERC Program which are ***directly complementary*** to
the recommendations regarding priorities for regional development
cooperation and investment of the multi-lateral working groups of

---

[4]   From early stages of the MERC program and until recently, *regional
cooperation* in MERC projects was in itself not easily accomplished and could not
be and was not taken for granted. Now, interest in regional cooperation even
among many countries of the Middle East themselves is expanding and deepening.
This welcome movement towards and acceptance of regional cooperation by the
parties who are the focus of the MERC Program allows the development contribution
of a MERC project to assume its major, proper importance.

-5-

the **Middle East Peace Process (MEPP), or other international fora similarly concerned with Middle East regional development cooperation,** *may have an advantage* when decisions are reached on allocations of available funds. Proposals without direct ties to or endorsement of such international fora are nonetheless encouraged and are fully eligible for consideration.

     E.   <u>**Non-traditional Projects.**</u> Although most MERC-supported activities resemble classical development projects in structure and purpose, the MERC Program is open for receipt of proposals of limited scope/scale and objectives when they involve special development opportunities and otherwise meet the MERC standards for regional cooperation. Such proposals must also address all relevant factors listed under the Guidelines (below). Proponents of such proposals should understand, however, that the MERC Program will use this flexibility on an exceptional rather than a regular basis.[5]

     F.   <u>**Receipt and Review of Proposals.**</u> *Preliminary proposals or "preproposals" (cf. III. Guidelines for Preliminary Proposals, below)* will be received and acknowledged by the USAID MERC program at any time. Full proposals may be invited by the MERC Program Executive Review Committee after favorable review of preproposals. Formal reviews of preproposals and invited full proposals are held at varying points each fiscal year depending on availability of funds, emerging political/developmental priorities, and number of preproposals received. Decisions of the MERC Program Executive Review Committee are communicated to preproposal/proposal sponsors approximately 45 days after review meetings. Sponsors of proposals judged by the USAID MERC Program to be of sufficient priority to warrant allocation of available funds are selected for negotiation of potential grant agreements. Grants are awarded when the terms of the grant have been agreed to. Grantees are responsible for administering grants in accordance with their terms and conditions, and in compliance with applicable U.S. laws and regulations.

---

    [5] An example of such activities could be a time-critical study, expert consultancy, or conference/symposium on an important matter which would set the stage for, if not also initiate, subsequent substantive regional cooperation on the priority topic.

Appendix D

A Survey of External Views/Assessments of the Cooperative Marine Technology Program for the Middle East

Possibly the most dramatic single aspect of what has always been a dramatic program has been the shift in the Arab attitude toward, first, cooperation with Israel, and then, the entire peace process. The first meetings were conducted in back rooms in Cairo (Egyptians simply could/ would not travel to Israel) hotels. As has been stated previously, the Egyptians' actions could be used reliably as a barometer of the progress of peace.

Significantly, therefore, it was at a meeting at the Israeli Institute of Oceanographic and Limnological Research that the Egyptians first suggested the accomplishment of this book, the principal component of which would be the "reminiscences of officials and dignitaries associated—or at least closely aware of—the Program." In order to avoid the appearance of a "Love Feast," a standard survey was prepared, finally receiving agreement of the Middle East participants.

The following papers reflect the perception of this trail-breaking component of the MERC program, in the eyes of persons of both authority and responsibility, especially responsibility for the overarching issues in the international peace process.

It is emphasized that these papers are included verbatim and do not reflect the opinions of the Program participants themselves, and especially, the author.

**Questions respecting the correspondent's views
of the Cooperative Marine Technology Program for the Middle East**
(Impressions and Reminiscences of the Program)

1. What were the circumstances of your first knowledge of, and/or
    interaction with, the Program? Who were the first person(s) with whom
    you spoke about the Program? What was the general nature of the discus-
    sion at that time?

2. What has been the nature of your involvement with the Program since
    that time? Have you received information about the Program since your
    first involvement?

3. Are you in accord with the fundamental principle of Regional
    Cooperation, i.e. getting previously hostile peoples to work together
    for their mutual benefit?

4. Do you believe this approach can be a positive factor in tension
    reduction, with particular reference to the Middle East?

5. Have you the perspective in which to judge the relative merits of the
    marine programs vis-a-vis the other project components of the Regional
    Cooperation Program? If so - how would you compare our efforts in
    terms of:

          a.   attaining cooperation
          b.   economic achievement
          c.   scientific achievement

6. In the above connection, in terms of 100%-whole, what percent
    importance would you assign to these three objectives?

7. What is your opinion, if any, about the progress the Program has made
    over the last ten years? What do you believe to have been the
    Program's principal products, services, and achievements?

8. How do you feel about introducing additional Arab Nations to the
    Program?

9. If you are in favor, how do you propose that we go about recruiting
    those countries?

10. Where do you think the Program should be going from here?

11. Do you believe the United States should expand its support of this
    Program?

12. Are there certain persons whom you believe ought to be involved in the
    Program, who are not currently participating?

Page (2)

13. Have you any recommendations to offer regarding selection of the projects, referring to the second enclosure?

14. Have you any recommendations to offer - respecting management of the marine program by its director and steering committee?

15. Have you any recommendations to offer respecting Federal Agency management of the Regional Cooperation Program?

16. Would you like to be kept better informed of the Program?

Please do not hesitate to change these questions in any way or to add further questions, if desired. I would appreciate being informed of these changes so that we may all share in them and that we may have as productive a discussion as possible at our next meeting.

One Hundredth Congress
Congress of the United States
Committee on Foreign Affairs
House of Representatives
Washington, DC 20515

November 10, 1988

Mr. Robert B. Abel
President
New Jersey Marine Sciences Consortium
Box 549
Marmora, New Jersey 08223

Dear Mr. Abel:

Thank you for your recent letter bringing me up to date on the status of the Cooperative Marine Technology Program for the Middle East. I appreciate having the benefit of this progress report.

I was pleased to learn that Egyptian-Israeli cooperation, particularly in the area of waste water utilization and recycling, is improving. The need for improvements in this area is long overdue.

The foreign assistance budget for fiscal year 1990 is currently under review within the Executive branch, and it is unclear what funding would be available for projects of this type. Nonetheless, should this issue come before the Committee in its processing of the foreign aid legislation next year, I will continue to give this program my close attention.

With best wishes, I am

Sincerely yours,

Dante B. Fascell
Chairman

DBF:rhd

Congress of the United States
Committee on Foreign Affairs
House of Representatives
Washington, D.C. 20515

September 20, 1982

Robert B. Abel
President
New Jersey Marine Sciences
  Consortium
Box 549
Marmora, New Jersey 08223

Dear Dr. Abel:

I appreciated your letter of September 13, 1982 regarding your important work with Israeli and Egyptian scientists involved in the marine technology program financed by AID.

I want to express my appreciation to you for keeping the subcommittee and its staff informed of your project and its progress. The seeds you are helping to plant to encourage broader and deeper Arab-Israeli cooperation are very important and such programs are strongly supported by the Congress. While in the present budget crunch, funds will be scarce, you can be sure that Congress will make its best efforts to insure that funds continue to be available to promote regional cooperative programs in the Middle East.

I wish you continued success and hope you will stay in touch with the subcommittee.

With best regards,

Sincerely yours,

Lee H. Hamilton
Chairman
Subcommittee on Europe
  and the Middle East

LHH:mvdr

United States Senate

COMMITTEE ON FOREIGN RELATIONS

WASHINGTON, D.C. 20510

February 16, 1984

Dr. Robert B. Abel
President
New Jersey Marine Sciences
   Consortium
Box 549
Marmora, New Jersey 08223

Dear Bob:

Thank you for your thoughtful letter of February 8 with the report on progress of the Cooperative Marine Technology Program for the Middle East.

The Cooperative Program stands as a unique achievement, both scientifically and diplomatically, in the Middle East. It is, as you know, the only such program in existence involving Israel and an Arab nation. The program can be justified solely on the basis of its scientific work, contributing to a solution of economic and environmental problems in the region. Equally important, however, is the outstanding success of the Program in developing mutual respect, understanding and cooperation in a region torn by religious, ethnic and nationalistic conflict.

I congratulate you on the progress of the program to date and wish you continued success.

The New Jersey Marine Sciences Consortium and, indeed, the State of New Jersey have reason to be proud of the essential leadership being provided in the development and implementation of the program. This achievement, in my view, can only add to the reputation, in the governmental, scientific and academic communities, of the New Jersey Marine Sciences Consortium.

With every good wish.

Ever sincerely,

Claiborne Pell

FRANK R. LAUTENBERG
NEW JERSEY

COMMITTEE:
APPROPRIATIONS

SUBCOMMITTEES:
TRANSPORTATION, CHAIRMAN
COMMERCE, JUSTICE, STATE AND JUDICIARY
DEFENSE
FOREIGN OPERATIONS
VA, HUD AND INDEPENDENT AGENCIES

COMMITTEE:
BUDGET

COMMITTEE:
ENVIRONMENT AND PUBLIC WORKS

SUBCOMMITTEES:
SUPERFUND, OCEAN AND WATER
PROTECTION, CHAIRMAN
ENVIRONMENTAL PROTECTION
WATER RESOURCES, TRANSPORTATION
AND INFRASTRUCTURE

HELSINKI COMMISSION

United States Senate

WASHINGTON, DC 20510-3002

August 10, 1992

Mr. Robert B. Abel
President
NJ Marine Sciences Consortium
Building 22
Executive Office
Fort Hancock, New Jersey   07732

Dear Bob:

Thanks for contacting me. I am pleased that the
United States Institute of Peace has awarded you a
grant to conduct research on the Cooperative Marine
Technology Program for the Middle East.

During my travels in the region, U.S. diplomats to
Israel and Egypt alike expressed to me that the Program
is helpful in easing the longstanding hostilities in
the region. Programs like this one can be useful in
creating a sense of cooperation and lessening tensions
and provide the kind of personal exposure to others
that is limited in the region. It also promotes
professional exchange of information that can be
beneficial throughout the Middle East.

Again, congratulations on your award. I hope the
Program continues to enjoy great success. I have
enclosed a copy of the letter I recently sent to
Senator Leahy urging him to provide $7 million for the
MERC program in fiscal year 1993. You know I'll
continue fighting for funds for this program.

Sincerely,

FRL:rms

Enclosure

REPLY TO:

☐ 506 HART SENATE OFFICE BUILDING
WASHINGTON, DC 20510-3002
(202) 224-4744

☐ ONE GATEWAY CENTER SUITE 1011
NEWARK, NEW JERSEY 07102-5311
(201) 645-3030

☐ BARRINGTON COMMONS
208 WHITE HORSE PIKE
SUITES 18-19
BARRINGTON, N.J. 08007-1322
(609) 757-5353

2408 RAYBURN HOUSE OFFICE BUILDING
WASHINGTON, DC 20515-0529
(202) 225-3976

DISTRICT OFFICE:
8436 WEST 3D STREET
SUITE 600
LOS ANGELES, CA 90048-4183
(213) 651-1040

COMMITTEES:
ENERGY AND COMMERCE
CHAIRMAN, SUBCOMMITTEE ON
HEALTH AND THE ENVIRONMENT

GOVERNMENT OPERATIONS

PHILIP M. SCHILIRO
ADMINISTRATIVE ASSISTANT

Congress of the United States
House of Representatives
Washington, DC 20515-0529

HENRY A. WAXMAN
29TH DISTRICT, CALIFORNIA

August 16, 1994

Dr. Robert B. Abel
Davidson Laboratory
711 Hudson Street
Hoboken, New Jersey 07030

Dear Dr. Abel:

I was sorry that I wasn't able to meet with you when you visited my office at the end of June, but was glad that you had an opportunity to speak with Russell Shaw of my staff. Russell told me about your conversation, and about the book that you have been commissioned to write on the Middle East Regional Cooperation Program (MERC).

One question which Russell said he wasn't able to answer during your meeting concerned the rationale behind establishing the MERC program. I will attempt to address that matter for you now. In the wake of the Camp David Peace Accords, policy makers were confronted with a new challenge--how could they break down the psychological barriers which had been built up between Arabs and Israelis, in order to form personal relationships which would be more durable than a peace treaty? It was in this context that I first conceived of the Middle East Regional Cooperation Program. By bringing scientists and researchers together to work on projects of mutual concern, it would be possible for Arabs and Israelis to transcend politics and develop real and lasting friendships.

An outside review of the MERC program conducted by Devres, Inc., and led by Ambassador C. William Kontos, determined in 1991: "The Middle East Regional Cooperation Program has achieved, during its ten years of existence, a remarkable record of success...In the entire range of USAID activities there are few programs in which foreign policy and developmental objectives have been matched so well as in the MERC." The MERC program has been so successful because of the unique role of scientific and technological cooperation in the program. Science, by its very nature, breaks down international barriers--when Arab and Israeli scientists work together they are able to see each other in a new and positive light.

Dr. Robert B. Abel
August 16, 1994
Page Two

     I look forward to reading your forthcoming publication, and wish you luck on its completion. Additionally, you can be sure that I will continue my strong support for scientific cooperation as a means of advancing the peace process in the Middle East.

     With kind regards, I am

                  Sincerely,

                  HENRY A. WAXMAN
                  Member of Congress

HAW:rhs

**AMBASSADOR OF
THE UNITED STATES OF AMERICA**

NEW DELHI

September 7, 1992

Dear Bob:

Your letter of July 22nd reached me here in New Delhi and I would be delighted to try to give you some thoughts on the program.

Having seen it develop from the early days, but at some distance, I am not sure that I can be totally effective. However, I will try on the attached piece of paper to give you a few responses and guide the answers to the questions by number.

With this letter come my thanks, and of course warm regards and good wishes,

Sincerely,

Thomas R. Pickering

Enclosure: a/s

Robert B. Abel,
    President,
        Executive Office,
            New Jersey Marine
                Sciences Consortium,
                    Building 22, Fort Hancock,
                        New Jersey 07732.

ENCLOSURE:

<u>ANALYSIS OF THE COOPERATIVE MARINE TECHNOLOGY PROGRAM</u>

<u>FOR THE MIDDLE EAST</u>

1.   I became aware of the program first in its early days
when I was Assistant Secretary in the State Department
for Oceans, Science and Environment in the late 1970's
and early 1980's.

2.   I believe that Bob Abel was probably the fellow who
spoke to me first about the program or probably wrote me
about it.

3.   I was generally supportive, having just completed a
tour of duty in Jordan, in hope that the program between
Israel and Egypt would gradually be moved in the
direction of including Jordan.

4.   I don't believe my permission was being requested for
the program although I was supportive.

5.   From time to time Bob Abel has kept in touch with me
about the program and its developments, most particularly
when I served as Ambassador to Israel between July 1985
and December 1988.

6.   Without having direct personal firsthand knowledge,
my feeling is that the program has made real progress,
both scientifically and in bringing further participants
together, in increasingly more productive and useful
interactions. A good individual to comment further might
be Mr. Anthony F. Rock, who was the Science Counselor in
Tel Aviv at the time, and who is currently at the United
States Mission to the European Communities in Brussels,
Belgium.

7.   I am generally favorable to the idea of introducing
additional Arab nations to the program as the peace
process and political atmosphere command. I would not
try to rush this part of the process, since the basis of
the program is scientific, not political.

8.   I believe that it would be important to seek the
support and help of the current Arab participants in the
program, and introducing other Arab states to its virtue,
accomplishments and rewards.

9.   I believe the new program should continue to
strenghen its scientific cooperative bases and expand the
fields in areas to include those that will be of most
interest to the widest number of Arab states. In this
regard, the environmental concerns are probably as high
on the list as many others.

-2-

10. I believe the United States should continue to be a
strong supporter of the program. Expansion should be
justified on the basis of scientific qualifications.
Money is short in the United States, and therefore the
program should be a strong competitor for enough funding
on the basis of its accomplishments and further prospects.

11. I have been far enough away from the current
management of the program not to be knowledgeable to make
a comment.

12. I would like to continue to be informed about the
program.

13. I have no suggestions to make.

ARAB REPUBLIC OF EGYPT

ACADEMY OF SCIENTIFIC RESEARCH AND TECHNOLOGY

101, KASR EL-EINI STREET, CAIRO.

July 11, 1986

Dr. Robert B. Abel
President
New Jersey Marine Sciences Consortium
Sandy Hook Executive Office
Building 22
Fort Hancock, N.J. 07732

Dear Bob:

On behelf of the Egyptian scientists and colleagues participating in the collaborative marine research program, we wish to express our appreciation and strong support for your efforts. These studies have been most beneficial on the scientific and technological aspects, as well as in promoting direct scientific interactions.

Your relentless efforts in managing and promoting this multidisciplinary research program are most impressive. We feel that this program will effectively satisfy the goals of the sponsoring agencies and, in particular, the U. S. Agency for International Development.

With all best wishes,

Sincerely,

A. F. Abdel Latif
Vice President

cc: Dr. K. H. Mancy
Dr. Sayed Z. El-Sayed
Dr. Refaet Bayoumi

**THE
GEORGE
WASHINGTON
UNIVERSITY**

Washington, D.C. 20052 / Graduate Program in Science, Technology, and Public Policy / (202) 676-7292

November 7, 1986.

Mr. Robert B. Abel, President
New Jersey Marine Sciences Consortium
Sandy Hook Executive Office
Building 22, Ft. Hancock, N. J. 07732

Dear Bob:

Thank you for sending me the trip reports and the proposed
agenda for the October 14 meeting. I am truly impressed by the
fact that your program is not only alive but seems to be thriving,
and by your apparently inexhaustible ability to surmount time
after time political, economic and other un-natural calamities.
Were it not for your determination and dedication, not to mention
your ingenuity and diplomatic skill, this program would have
long since died on the vine. I cannot offer any suggestions
that would be helpful to you because it seems to me that you are
doing everything that can possibly be done. Keep it up!

All the best.

Sincerely,

Herman Pollack
Research Professor of
International Affairs